T0116898

Our Inactive Medical and Judicial Systems

How to Litigate Against an Incompetent Attorney

Mary Sansiviero

authorHOUSE®

AuthorHouse™
1663 Liberty Drive
Bloomington, IN 47403
www.authorhouse.com
Phone: 1-800-839-8640

Published by AuthorHouse   04/23/2012

ISBN: 978-1-4567-5712-0 (e)
ISBN: 978-1-4567-5714-4 (sc)

Library of Congress Control Number: 2011904749

Print information available on the last page.

Any people depicted in stock imagery provided by Thinkstock are models, and such images are being used for illustrative purposes only.
Certain stock imagery © Thinkstock.

This book is printed on acid-free paper.

Because of the dynamic nature of the Internet, any web addresses or links contained in this book may have changed since publication and may no longer be valid. The views expressed in this work are solely those of the author and do not necessarily reflect the views of the publisher, and the publisher hereby disclaims any responsibility for them.

DEDICATION

This Book is dedicated to the unsuspecting public, to the disabled and those who have been reduced to invalid status, who have been victimized and/or traumatized by our medical and judicial systems.

Special thanks to my loyal family and friends for their continuous outpouring of love and support.

FOREWORD

Please note, for "obvious reasons"
most of the names contained in
this narrative, are fictitious.

* * *

DISCLAIMER:

This book is not intended to give
legal advice or counsel. It is
simply a description of the
author's experience. It is in no
way intended to substitute for
competent legal advice or counsel.

The Accident

The true story you are about to read is an attempt by the writer to balance the unplanned, deep challenges faced when thrown into the legal and medical arenas. The writer will give a blistering account of her struggle against injustice due to legal and medical incompetence. I hope that this true story will continue to remain a harsh reminder of just how vulnerable we, the public, are in the hands of our medical and judicial systems. Trusting this narrative will be timely for those who are presently involved in litigation or who may very well become involved in the future.

To those *caring, competent and well-meaning physicians and attorneys* who do indeed exist, I sincerely regret having to make this admonishment.

While driving to work on a snowy day in February of 1980, a Fleetwood Cadillac skidded over to my side of the road and collided with the front of my automobile. Immediately thereafter, I experienced twisting and swirling movements of my head and the *"sensation"* of something encasing my brain. I sought medical attention and informed my treating physician that, in my opinion, my symptoms were caused by my upper left tooth, having experienced a toothache earlier that morning. My physician, Doctor Gram, then suggested that I visit two dentists who, after examination, both concluded my medical problem was not caused by my tooth, although the tooth had to be extracted. Doctor Gram then informed me he did not know whether the symptoms I was describing were caused by my tooth or shock.

When we are in indescribable, torturous pain, we tend to accept the recommendations and conclusions of recognized medical experts, because we want them to bring about a cure.

Prior to any medication having been prescribed, I experienced a *"sensation"* of a bag of cement hardening around my brain *(included in my daily log),* and continuing to increase in intensity with swelling about my face and skull.

Doctor Gram then recommended that I maintain a daily log; he stated: *"Dentists aren't always right."* Years later that daily log was the key to the diagnosis of the bizarre enigma. A careful study of the log by the physicians would have given them beneficial insight into the diagnosis of a most immeasurably torturous medical problem. A short time later, I contacted one dentist again to ascertain if it was at all possible that my medical condition could be caused by my upper left tooth. He again reiterated his original conclusion that it was definitely not caused by my tooth.

Later, I regurgitated, felt weak and exhibited some symptoms but on formal examination, I did not demonstrate any physical signs of head injury.

The pains continued to increase as if I were on a roller coaster. My treating physician, Doctor Gram, recommended an orthopedic surgeon who prescribed an anti-inflammatory medication, which ultimately caused violent disabling effects upon my body. He indicated in his medical report that *the patient was treated conservatively with anti-inflammatory medication.*

Doctor Gram was very much aware of the extensive swellings throughout my body and the gastrointestinal problems. I queried him as to why the orthopedist would include the word *"Conservatively"* when I had experienced such a violent reaction to the medication; whereupon, he stated, "He included that statement because he did not want to be sued for medical malpractice." We all realize that medications have served to help many of us. However, when physicians administer medications without understanding their violent disabling effects, the results can be deadly.

Thereafter, Doctor Gram submitted a report to the drug company concerning my adverse reaction to the first medication which was prescribed. Two other anti-inflammatory medications with adverse reactions were also prescribed. It was then recommended by Doctor Gram and the orthopedist that I seek a neurologist -- my legs had buckled, I lost my balance and bounced against the wall. The initial neurologist, Doctor Lotta, was very brusque and aggressive, lifting my right arm over my head in a quick, sudden and unexpected manner. There was a rapid, irregular "giving-way" on direct muscle testing, consistent with functional "giving-way." Tears rolled down my cheeks from the pain he inflicted. He then attempted to feel my neck and raise my left arm; I informed him he was not going to inflict any more pain on me. Doctor Lotta dismissed my complaints as inconsequential. His medical report cited me as a *"good historian."* There was a failure to be understood or treated. I complained of my lower legs and Doctor Lotta recommended that I confer with a rheumatoid specialist. He proceeded to dictate his medical report in my presence and, after I corrected him on three separate occasions, he aggressively and angrily stated *"You're not going to get a penny from this case."*

As a patient, you should be impressed by a physician's learned posture of his diagnosis but, unfortunately, that was not the case. Indeed what is said by the patient is ignored. I thought the medications were causing my dizziness, recurring nausea and retching. I stopped the medications, but I continued to experience dizziness, nausea and retching.

In this golden age of medical technology, public expectations of the medical community are very high and we must rid ourselves of those high expectations.

In the mornings, I was literally unable to rise from the bed. I had to slide out on my knees and crawl to the commode. Needless to say, I spent most of my time in bed. Doctor Gram then recommended that I visit another neurologist. I made an appointment with Doctor Maylin who seemed very understanding and compassionate, but who stated in his medical report, "Has only occasional headaches and dizziness." I informed him that I had torturous head pain and the only thing that changed was its intensity. I felt as though I had a clamp on my head, and wanted to put my head through a pencil sharpener. Doctor Maylin's medical report also stated that there had been no associated fevers. My treating physician Doctor Gram had witnessed low-grade fevers over many years. At my direction, Mr. Judas, my attorney, sent a letter to Doctor Maylin regarding these errors. Doctor Maylin also ordered an electroencephalogram with the results being "essentially normal." Thereafter, Doctor Maylin informed me that I was experiencing anxiety due to litigation. During my last visit to his office he asked, *"who gave you permission to remain at home?"* Pointing to my chest, I stated as loudly and as succinctly as I could, *"I did."* Wherein Doctor Maylin remained silent.

In July of 1980, I visited Doctor Feilman, a physician from my insurance carrier. When I entered the room, he exclaimed in a shocked tone of voice, "Oh my God!" His report later indicated that I was unable to work, "she has Hyporreflexia." Two other physicians indicated the correct spelling was H-Y-P-E-R-R-E-F-L-E-X-I-A, because I was experiencing exaggerated reflexes.

In September of 1980, I visited a second physician from my insurance carrier, Doctor Morsey. His medical report stated "Doctor Feilman's comment that the patient *"may"* have Hyperreflexia is not a diagnosis that I would use." Doctor Feilman never used the word *"may"* but wrote, *"She has Hyperreflexia."* The Hyperreflexia had subsided prior to my visit to Dr. Morsey's office in September, but my treating physician, Doctor Gram, substantiated that diagnosis in July of 1980.

Doctor Morsey also stated in his report, *"No nystagmus."* Doctor Gram informed me he was only able to recognize nystagmus when I was sitting up, but the audiological and electromyography tests indicated that there was direction-changing nystagmus (A rapid, involuntary, oscillatory motion of the eyeball). I was groggy from the medication and Doctor Gram was aware of this fact; my daily log also substantiated this reaction. Doctor Morsey stated, "Profound depression. It is not all from the accident. I do feel she should be seen by a psychiatrist." He was unable to diagnose the symptomology of allergenic reactions to medications. In another statement cited in his report, "At no time did she lose her balance." I lost my balance numerous times, all being documented by my full office medical records and hospital records. As a result of Doctor Morsey's negative medical report, my no-fault benefits were cancelled in

September of 1980 at which time I was reduced to invalid status while in torturous unrelenting pain. His medical report reflected that all the medical reports from the other examining physicians, in addition to my full office medical records, were not in his possession. How else could Doctor Morsey deal with his frustration over his own incompetence and his powerlessness in diagnosing an elusive disorder?

Before leaving Doctor Morsey's office, I asked, "What is wrong with me?" He stated, "I don't know."

Second-class medical attention always eats at one's dignity! Physicians should be concerned with the implications of their actions and the impact they have on their patients. Doctor Morsey did not know whether there was really a neurological deficit causing the problem; head injury is just not understood. He was medically intolerant and indifferent towards me and displayed a deplorable lack of sensitivity with an attitude of superiority. We are all frostbitten by life, but Dr. Morsey failed to take the reasonable precautions, which is indicative of *"a lack of common sense."* Apparently, like other incompetent physicians, paid for and retained by insurance companies, he was unable to grasp the overall consequences of failing to meet requirements, their inadequate ability and their incompetence; therefore, they should be notified and taught. You would be amazed at the volume of mistakes made by physicians who are still practicing, and their incompetence is aggravated by their aggressive manner.

When my attorney sent Doctor Morsey's medical report to my home, I informed Doctor Gram of the physician's decision contained in his report, which stated: "I do feel she should be seen by a psychiatrist." I relayed this recommendation by the neurologist to Doctor Gram who laughed loudly and stated, "I am a psychiatrist; psychiatry was a previous specialty of mine." I was quite surprised by Doctor Gram's revelation inasmuch as I had visited him in the past for nutritional purposes only. Then he made a tight fist at his chest and thrust it forward in a quick fashion stating, *"Not only don't you need a psychiatrist, you are a bulldozer. You are the most lucid person I know. I wouldn't waste my time or the insurance company's money."*

Who is responsible for doctors enjoying the "revolving door syndrome," better known as allowing doctors to pass through the revolving door in our society? For those who are not aware, it is the *"establishment,"* the inadequate, inactive, enormously wealthy medical societies who do not help shape their practice and do not perceive it as destructively or morally wrong to persist in failure, error, transgression of duty and deceptions; *The medical process works in favor of the Insurance Physicians.*

Doctor Morsey and the other incompetent insurance physicians have literally slipped through the cracks, gotten away with incompetence, had caused very severe complications to someone suffering from absolute torture, and ultimately caused our judicial system to expend enormous monies because of their incompetence. I trust you will not be that next victim of any doctor's irresponsibility and callousness; this degree of incompetence and arrogance must not go unpunished and the public must be made aware of such happenings.

This true story is not aimed at condemnation, but *at the need for change within the medical process.* We, the public, are not requesting physician license forfeiture; on the other hand, we want to be protected from those physicians who do not care, have no value system, or are unwilling to admit to their blundering errors. In order to do that, the medical system must use an antiseptic-type of cleansing process. The most powerful and effective manner of controlling physicians who have either made gross errors or violated ethical considerations would be a requirement that they be a speaker at a medical teaching college or university every month for one semester or be a speaker at seminars for physicians or future physicians. There is no better teacher for medical students than those who have made blundering errors. Medical errors must be exposed for the benefit of the public; you are dealing with human lives. How dare you do otherwise!

You cannot distance yourself from this true story without having your own legal and medical rights infringed upon.

Each time I took a painkiller, my eyes became groggy and Doctor Gram was aware of this problem. Eventually, he recommended that all medications be discontinued. He indicated it was difficult for him to distinguish whether the grogginess was from the medication or the accident.

My symptoms worsened following physical therapy and chiropractic treatments. A therapist at the hospital caught me just prior to my falling and placed me in a wheelchair.

Doctor Gram, who was not connected with any hospital stated: *"You belong in a hospital,"* witnessing that the neurological problem was worsening. He recommended no further chiropractic or physical therapy treatments until such time as my body would be able to tolerate such procedures. He then suggested that a member of my family "lightly" apply a hydroculator and an oster vibrator to my back and neck. Doctor Fegrina, the first chiropractor, reported, "No further treatments were needed." His report also remarked that I had consulted with a Doctor Leim, a mistake, since I had never seen a Doctor Leim. Apparently my file had been confused with another file.

Subsequently, Doctor Fegrina's report was corrected to *"further treatments were needed,"* but this was only *"after"* the adverse decision was rendered by the original Tribunal. Prior to the original tribunal, Mr. Judas, my attorney, had never discussed Doctor Fegrina's negative report with me.

In September of 1980, I visited Doctor Nat, a physician paid for and retained by the insurance company for my personal disability policy, and I informed him that in the "morning" I had regurgitated. His report stated: "In the afternoon she claimed that she felt weak and began throwing up." Also contained in that report, he stated: "It appears to be drug induced." Doctor Nat was unable to diagnose a cyanotic condition *(A bluish discoloration of the skin and finger nails)* which was confirmed by two other physicians in addition to my daily log. His medical report further stated: "I feel that this patient is capable of returning to work on a part-time basis in her capacity of court stenographer as of October 1, 1980." He did not believe that I was in torturous pain and found it very difficult even to sit up. Doctor Nat had a condescending smirk from ear to ear while examining and conversing with me. I advised the manager of the insurance company of the manner in which I was treated and he became very angry and indicated he would call the physician. Thereafter, an insurance company agent arrived at my home unexpectedly and inquired sarcastically, *"What are you doing there in bed?"* A short time later, benefits were cancelled by my insurance carrier while I was reduced to invalid status and in indescribable torturous pain with absolutely no income.

Physicians should be forced to take a sensitivity training course once a year because when we, the public, visit a physician, we should not have to put up with their behavioral problems.

The following is a list of the medical problems I had incurred:

- Severe vertigo   - violent reactions to medications

- Pains all over my body

- Cerebella ataxia   - Hyperreflexia

- Sciatica in both legs - nausea

- Torturous unrelenting head pains

- continuous severe neurological problems

- Involuntary movements

- Imbalance

- Noise and light sensitivity

- Extreme weakness to extreme exhaustion

- Collapsing

- Direction-changing nystagmus

- Wiggling Posture   - low-grade fevers

- Severe distension of the abdomen

- Poor hearing   - reverberating

- visual problems   - Room spinning

- Acute labyrinthitis

- very severe sleeping difficulties

- Disjointed ankles   - severe, neck,
                             back, shoulders,
                             wrists,and groin
                             discomfort

- Huge mounds on upper chest

- lumps on the sides of my neck,

I was totally dependent on others for my care, reduced to invalid status and spending most of my time in bed. I experienced violent reactions to three medications. I became jaundiced with severe swellings throughout my body, severe diarrhea, cyanotic condition (finger nails were bluish in color), and severe widening of my eyelids. Medications had affected my liver, kidney, bladder and pancreas, and eventually persistent cerebella ataxia (uncoordinated muscle movements).

My liver swelled as a result of the reaction to the medications, and tests revealed there was, in fact, a liver problem.

Medication was later prescribed to curtail the room-spinning, positional vertigo and acute labyrinthitis (severe dizziness). Doctor Gram suggested talking books and recommended I use a wheelchair for any outside medical appointments due to my falling and possible self-injury.

There was also distention of my upper and lower stomach to enormous proportions until 1995.

And Doctor Nat stated in his medical report: *"I feel that this patient is capable of returning to work on a part-time basis…."*

We, the public, are not provided any protection from irresponsible and incompetent professionals; *they* are provided protection.

Since I was continuing to experience severe diarrhea due to the violent disabling reactions to medications, Doctor Gram recommended a gastroenterologist who prescribed a medication which caused an itch and dry mouth. Subsequently, it was recommended that the medication be discontinued. I informed the gastroenterologist that the diarrhea was caused by the medication prescribed by the orthopedist.

In his first medical report, the gastroenterologist stated that the treatment rendered during her office visits was not related to any injury sustained from her involvement in a car accident. I asked Doctor Gram why the gastroenterologist did not indicate that the diarrhea was due to the medication as I informed him, and Doctor Gram responded, "Because he was more concerned about you litigating against the orthopedist who prescribed the medication than you."

Years later, with much effort, the gastroenterologist submitted a second report: "It is unknown whether her condition is as a result of the reactions to medications or as a result of the automobile accident."

In November of 1980, upon the recommendation of the first neurologist, I visited a rheumatologist. He prescribed a medication which my treating physician strongly advised I not take. I complained to the rheumatologist of my lower legs, but he said there was nothing wrong with my lower legs. A short time later in early 1981, Doctor Messe, a chiropractor stated: "You have disjointed ankles." My eyelids continued to "widen" and the indescribable pains in my head remained constant.

In November of 1980, a hematologist in his report indicated, "Her abdomen showed no masses." I found his determination unbelievable inasmuch as he never palpated my abdomen! "Her extremities were without cyanosis."

At this time, Doctor Gram recommended the Holistic Center because of the obvious cyanotic condition. The hematologist report indicated: "On physical examination, we could find no abnormalities. Diagnosis: Symptomatic relief." Doctor Gram definitely disagreed, stating: "I am sorry for the error, Miss Mary, because there is no doubt in my mind that your body is full of toxins."

Prior to my visit to the Holistic Center, the wiggling posture had subsided. Doctor Bovitz at the center recommended a substance called *"Green Clay,"* a purifying agent for the cyanotic condition. Within a couple of days, a pus-like substance was secreted furiously through the mouth coupled with an increase of excruciating pains throughout my body, quivering and shaking and the pulling and drawing throughout my body.

The cyanotic condition, leaky bladder, severe diarrhea and "widening of my eyes" subsided *(included in my daily log)*. The "depressed appearance" of my eyes no longer existed. Thereafter the toxins were secreted intermittently through the mouth and stool, but very slowly.

The center's report contained this statement: "The distention of the upper and lower stomach," which continued to increase to enormous proportions until 1995. Doctor Bovitz' medical report also stated that I was given a "placebo," but subsequently a member of the center's medical personnel informed me that that was an error, since Green Clay was not a placebo but a purifying agent. I informed Mr. Judas, my attorney, of this error wherein he commented: "It's better if the error remains."

When it was obvious that my attorney was not going to make the necessary correction, I contacted Doctor Bovitz regarding the error. He immediately advised Mr. Judas in writing that "The word 'placebo' was inadvertent and erroneous."

A brain scan was then ordered by Doctor Bovitz. I reacted with hives as a result of the dye injected for the scan. Also, unbeknownst to me, the residue of the toxins remained in my system and hardened throughout my body; this was later confirmed by a sophisticated test which was performed in 1995.

Following treatment at the Holistic Center, Doctor Gram recommended that antibiotic therapy be used interchangeably with the purifying agent, Green Clay. As a result, pus continued to be secreted very slowly and intermittently through the mouth and stool.

I continued to spend most of the time confined to my bed in torturous, indescribable pain for twenty-one years. It felt as though a bag of cement had hardened around my brain, and this was the description contained in my daily log. I experienced severe pains all over my body. Every movement such as a mere turning in bed would increase the acute pain.

In May of 1981, the room would not stop spinning and the retching, regurgitating, and falling to the floor continued. At the direction of Doctor Lauria, I was taken by ambulance to the hospital and in the emergency room, he exclaimed: "There is nothing wrong with you." I responded in no uncertain terms: "I'm not leaving this hospital until you find out what is wrong with me." He then asked if I wanted a specialist and I replied, "Yes."

Doctor Teeman, the specialist, looked into my eyes and informed Doctor Lauria, "This woman belongs in a hospital." At this point both physicians walked behind a nearby curtain and almost immediately a nurse pushed my gurney towards that very curtain to accommodate another patient. I overheard Doctor Teeman state: *"This woman belongs in a hospital,"* but Doctor Lauria answered, "No, she is an accident case."

Whatever happened to the *Hippocratic Oath?* I was informed later that the doctors just did not want to be "dragged" into court to testify. Physicians, you must realize that this comes with your territory. This is what is commonly referred to as interference with the treatment of a patient; in a hospital the patient is irrelevant. My inner activity was one of intense struggle and frustration; the frustration was almost more than I could bear.

Both physicians prescribed Antivert for the room-spinning, and Doctor Teeman instructed me to call him if the Antivert did not relieve this problem. I was experiencing absolute torture, but I was still released from the hospital.

We must raise our awareness of these situations because they can very easily affect you and your family.

A short time after taking the Antivert, the pains increased to such magnitude that I was literally unable to move. Drippings came down the back of my neck and torturous agonizing head pains became even more torturous and indescribable, all this being noted in my daily log. Following the "drippings" down the back of my neck, the Antivert was positive in that the spinning of the room completely subsided. Diagnosis: Acute labyrinthitis, positional vertigo.

Subsequently I called Doctor Teeman and explained to him that my initial complaint to Doctor Gram, my treating physician, was the *"sensation"* of something encasing my brain and I *"strongly felt"* it was from my upper left tooth, but that was ruled out by two dentists. Doctor Teeman stated: "My diagnosis remains the same: acute labyrinthitis, positional vertigo." I also informed him that I was now experiencing "pulling, drawing and wind sensation in my head," which I "strongly felt" was the reaction to the Antivert. He laughed loudly, and wanted to know what Medical College I attended. I was severely criticized and I was in profound torture, but I was dismissed. I was in bitter agony and I was met with scorn and derision. I had now made the mistake of "assuming" that the specialist was correct, that the "pulling, drawing and wind sensation" were not caused by the Antivert. However, I included these symptoms in my daily log, which was not examined by any physician until many years later. Every neurologist and physician had stated, in words or substance, in their reports that there was no disturbed recent or long-term memory.

In order to allot a patient full concern and benefit, there should be a stronger interaction between physicians. It is commonly recognized that different physicians have a different set of assumptions accepted as a basis for reasoning, but physicians must communicate very carefully with other physicians and their patients. In that way, their mistakes may be eliminated by double-checking. Doctor Gram informed me that the only time a neurologist had contacted him was for the purpose of confrontation.

Thereafter I visited Doctor Kenyon, a neurologist, a physician paid for and retained by the insurance company. My attorney, Mr. Judas, instructed me to inform him that I was receiving psychiatric treatments from Doctor Gram, my treating physician, and I refused. I informed Doctor Kenyon that I had been given a shot of Dramamine, but he stated in his report; "Intramuscular Valium." The hospital report stated that the patient was given a shot of "Dramamine." Also included in his report was the statement: "Unknown whether the symptoms were from the *idiosyncratic responses* to medications."

Eventually I was unable to either read or write. One day Doctor Gram requested that I read a paragraph in his presence, and he witnessed that I was just about able to speak.

My no-fault benefits were cancelled in September of 1980. I continuously asked Mr. Judas, my attorney, to assist me in obtaining a reinstatement, but he waited one year before he took any action for a hearing.

Prior to the original Tribunal in 1981, Mr. Judas insisted upon dictating a paragraph over the telephone of our intent to appeal Doctor Morsey's negative decision (my insurance carrier physician). When I refused because of my torturous agonizing pains, he became very aggressive and loud. Two people then held me up in a chair as he dictated the paragraph of our intention to appeal; a typist then transcribed the very short paragraph from my notes. Mr. Judas did not believe that I was in torturous agonizing pain. It was brought to my attention years later that he never requested my full office medical records from Doctor Gram, my treating physician, until many years later.

Immediately prior to the original Tribunal, I had requested Mr. Judas to subpoena all my physicians; this request was not granted. I requested that he at least call my treating physician; this was also ignored.

During this time I was experiencing intermittent cerebella ataxia. In August of 1981, in the anteroom of the original Tribunal, I was lying on a bench when Mr. Judas walked up to me and sneered, snickered and made faces in a very condescending manner. Was he angry because I kept insisting that my physicians be present at the Tribunal? Was he angry because I was constantly reminding him of the medical reports? While still in the anteroom, he flipped through a couple of medical reports and said, "This case is a piece of s_ _ _."

The original Tribunal lasted less then ten minutes. Mr. Judas did not adhere to the following procedural requirements:

1. He did not subpoena and cross-examine the two physicians who could have been presented by the other side.

2. He did not present medical testimony in support of my enormous personal injuries.

3. He did not submit a brief on the medical facts.

4. He did not submit a brief on the law regarding the responsibility and casual

relationship of allergenic reactions to medications.

5. He did not submit highly significant and material medical reports. Consequently, all of the plaintiff's enormous personal injuries were not submitted to the Tribunal.

6. He did not advise the panel that the medical problem of hyperreflexia had subsided prior to my visit in September of 1980 to Doctor Morsey, my insurance carrier's physician.

7. He did not advise the panel that my cyanotic condition, leaky bladder, widening of my eyes, and the "*depressed appearance*" of my eyes had subsided following treatment at the Holistic Center.

Being inadequately prepared, Mr. Judas deprived that original Tribunal of pertinent material evidence essential for a positive outcome. An unbelievable pattern of irresponsibility and lack of preparation.

At his Examination Before Trial, Mr. Judas testified under oath: "I felt my representation of the plaintiff was good. I don't conceive that any errors were made. At that point in time, I thought whatever I did was proper."

Q. What was your professional judgment at that time as to how to handle that proceeding?

A. The way we handled it. As far as I am concerned, no error was made."

Mr. Judas stood up at the Original Tribunal and said: "My client has been receiving psychiatric treatments." I attempted to correct his blundering error, but the middle doctor, Doctor Meika stated: "After speaking with this woman, it is obvious that she did not need these psychiatric treatments." When, in fact, I was never, at any time, treated under said specialty! Apparently, Mr. Judas assumed that Doctor Morsey was correct when he was unable to diagnose the symptomology of allergenic reactions to medications. My attorney did not do his homework.

Visibly upset, I contacted Doctor Gram, my treating physician, and informed him that my attorney, Mr. Judas, had misrepresented me at the Original Tribunal by erroneously stating that I was receiving psychiatric treatments. Doctor Gram then exclaimed: *"You tell your lawyer to call me, and soon."* I left a message at Mr. Judas' office requesting that he call Doctor Gram. Following their conversation, the doctor informed me that I was indeed correct, that Mr. Judas admitted he was under the misapprehension that I was receiving psychiatric treatments. Within days of their conversation, Mr. Judas began to berate me in a manner only a lawyer could when he knows he had made grave errors. The information he received from Doctor Gram triggered his outright aggression; he could not bear reality. He commenced a massive hard-hitting verbal personal attack on me while I was reduced to invalid status in indescribable agonizing torture. He became ballistic, loud, used acidic language coupled with sarcasm; he was degrading, demeaning, offensive; his dialogue was cutting and biting; his tone was intense and confrontational, commonly referred to as intimidation in an overbearing manner. I was brutalized.

In a loud, laughing, snickering and sarcastic tone of voice, Mr. Judas asked: "Why don't you get out of that bed? You're going to get so fat that you're not going to be able to walk. How is your mental condition? Are you taking

Valium yet?" He continued to be ruthless and manipulative. Doctor Gram never at any time prescribed Valium or any anti-depressant, and "strongly" advised against taking any medications that any other physician would prescribe due to the difficulty in diagnosis.

It was clear at the outset what my attorney was attempting to accomplish: He was trying to get rid of me. Being aware of the limited nature of review by the original Tribunal, he was attempting to maintain his position by external pressure and reduce me to an object. He engaged in this devious, well-planned effort while I was reduced to invalid status. He was chronically aggressive, similar to a "stealth bomber," all this occurring while I could not lift my head from the pillow, bearing in mind the slightest sound was a source of acute stress. He was attempting to deflect attention from his gross misrepresentation and thereby apply to withdraw due to the client/attorney relationship being deteriorated to the point that he could not represent me. Better known as a legal lynching!

There was an undeniably extreme, lengthy and bizarre campaign of harassment against me. What existed was an escalating power struggle which included unleashing his wrath, his harassment, his provocation, his manipulation and victimization, all of which continued until 1984.

Mr. Judas testified at his Examination Before Trial: "I have no recollection of ever attacking the plaintiff."

Ask yourself: What manner of man is it who hurls insults at his client who is reduced to invalid status? By his excessive harshness, we must assume that the constant and intense suffering of his client was of little or no concern to him.

At this point I contacted a neurologist, Doctor Maylin, who indicated that I was experiencing anxiety due to litigation. I explained the circumstances surrounding the misrepresentation of my attorney, and the doctor exclaimed: "Tell your lawyer to have the panel call me." This message was relayed to Mr. Judas who remarked cuttingly and bitingly, "You can't do that!" This was an attempt to conceal sensitive information. In the legal community, it is called non-disclosure. A legal dilemma indeed! I was informed years later that the error could have been easily remedied before the decision was rendered by the Original Tribunal.

Mr. Judas' secretary, Mona, continuously slammed down the telephone before I could even finish my inquiry. When I informed him of his secretary's behavior, his remark was: "If you don't like it, get yourself another lawyer."

Rather than applying for a rehearing within the arbitration system before the decision was rendered, due to an error in the description of writer's medical treatment, which was the proper course, Mr. Judas participated in the preservation of false evidence and a massive personal attack upon me.

He knowingly failed to disclose his misrepresentation of me, that medical reports were in transit, and that there were corrected medical reports which had not been submitted to the Original Tribunal. He was required by law to reveal these facts. When he did appeal to the Master Arbitrator, there were inadequate disclosures which disadvantaged me. He never sent the appeal to me prior to submitting the appeal to the Master Arbitrator. Non-disclosure is a violation of professional standards. My attorney was burying the truth, causing a blurring of the legal issues; he was attempting to conceal and suppress sensitive information that he had a legal obligation to produce. I requested that he make the necessary corrections, and he replied, "I can't do that; I have my reputation to think about." The Tribunal Administrator later informed me, *"Your attorney is aware of the remedies at his disposal."*

In the appeal Mr. Judas submitted an untruth: "Miss Sansiviero was the only person to give live testimony. They just wanted to hear what Miss Sansiviero had to say." The decision of the panel reads: "The panel reviewed evidence and took testimony of the applicant and her attorney." Following the adverse decision being rendered by the Master Arbitrator, I requested that Mr. Judas appeal and correct his errors and he responded, "Our office doesn't make mistakes." In addition, he informed me, *"It's better for your case if they think you are receiving psychiatric treatments."* I advised him that he had a stricture against judgment.

My attorney provided illegal guidance and became the lethal weapon in my legal matter. He refused to prepare an appeal following the adverse decision of the Master Arbitrator, and advised me in writing of a Mr. Booma, a so-called, well-respected appeal's attorney on Long Island.

After three telephone conversations, Mr. Booma informed me, *"Joseph said your case has no merit,"* and slammed down the telephone disconnecting our call. All this occurred while Mr. Judas remained my attorney of record. I then contacted several attorneys in an effort to retain counsel for the appeal of the Master Arbitrator's decision, but they all informed me in words or substance, "Your own attorney said your case has no merit and you are receiving psychiatric treatments. Furthermore, if you tell anyone what I said I will deny it." Another attorney indicated," If you tell anyone I will say I don't remember."

Bear in mind that Mr. Judas was privy to the fact that I was never at anytime treated under the specialty of psychiatry. This devious move by him was creating a powerful enough protection that I was at a point of diminished expectation that the truth would ever be submitted. I was confronted with my attorney's unmatched skills for deceit in attempting to protect himself and his position, but also trying to discourage other lawyers from taking my case. I was now placed in a position of attempting to overcome a major obstacle, the barrier of stigma, which my own attorney was intentionally placing upon me in his strong attempt to thwart the legal battle.

To my great disadvantage, Mr. Judas was exposing to public view that which he knew was a lie. There was no doubt in my mind that he was hoping his false statements would hold me up to ridicule, contempt or scorn or, better yet, public humiliation.

We should be very careful what we say about others since there is no guarantee that that which we ridicule in others, or lie about others, will not return to you and your family with greater magnitude. This is an example of professionals who make grave errors and attempt to do everything in their power to cover their blatant errors by deliberate wrongful conduct with no concern for the damage or consequences to others as long as they are not implicated.

The atmosphere was filled with relentless aggression while I was locked in a bitter legal battle. My own attorney, who was suppressing evidence, was denying my right to due process and causing incalculable damage; the writer became a victim of legal outrage by her own attorney. Deception and aggression were calculated to produce a maximum amount of anxiety and confusion. I now felt I was in the torture chamber of transformation.

Prior to the decision being rendered by the Master Arbitrator, I was scheduled to visit another neurologist, Doctor Menkel, in November of 1981. I advised Mr. Judas of such notice, but he did not request an extension in order to secure the medical report of that neurologist. While at Doctor Menkel's office, I was literally unable to remain seated and had to lie down on the couch due to the torturous, indescribable pains together with extreme exhaustion to near collapse. This neurologist had touching sensitivity and was very compassionate but unfortunately, unbeknownst to me, I was giving the symptoms descriptive of conversion hysteria (suggestive of a neurological problem). Doctor

Menke's report stated: "Largely somatic" (Physical). Suffering from anxiety due to litigation." A further report in 1996 stated: "In no way is this feigned or simulated."

Doctor Gram's medical report stated: "She has shown herself to be a remarkably well-balanced woman with an impeccable short-term and long-term memory." Mr. Judas, my attorney, responded to this report by stating, "We won't submit that report because it's better if they think you are receiving psychiatric treatments." I informed Mr. Judas his judgment is deemed impaired.

Initially Doctor Gram wanted me to write at least a short sentence each day, but there were numerous times when I could not even write a sentence without having someone holding me up. For many years, I was literally unable to read or write at all.

An appeal had to be submitted regarding the decision of the Master Arbitrator. Despite my body's failure to function and being reduced to invalid status and immeasurable agonizing torturous head pain and severe pains throughout my body, I requested legal stenographers to read to me aloud whatever portion of the file I had in my possession, but on numerous occasions I was literally unable to speak due to the torturous pain. The added pressure of dictating was overwhelming.

Lawyers supposedly have a very vital role in the legal process and this was major litigation. My rights were prejudiced and due process was unavailable since I was unaware of the legal elements of the problem and not trained in the subtleties of legal analysis. Mr. Judas by discouraging attorneys from handling my appeal complicated my legal situation because I did not have an attorney to guide me through the intricacies of the legal process.

Soon after the legal papers were sent to Mr. Judas by the legal stenographers, including his gross errors, he became even more livid and increased his massive personal attack on me; I was bitterly contested by my own attorney. Indeed, this was a period of enormous inner struggle.

Due to the fact that my head pains were so indescribably agonizing and so constant, I called Doctor Maylin, the neurologist, and asked in a loud voice, "What is wrong with me? Everybody is telling me something different." His reply was: "Anxiety due to litigation." It had come to my attention that there had been a confrontation between neurologist Doctor Maylin and Doctor Gram, my treating physician, because they disagreed as to the diagnosis.

Eventually another hearing was scheduled before Referee Switt regarding back disability. Mr. Judas called me from Riverhead Courthouse and instructed me to call Doctor Maylin and tell him it was not necessary for him to appear and testify. Thereupon, I called the referee who stated that he disagreed with my attorney, "The more evidence the better." Apparently an honest referee!

Later that day, "Monte," my cousin-attorney from Maryland, contacted me and after explaining the circumstances to him, stated: "Mary, you are so naïve. Your own lawyer wants to present a losing case because he lost at the Original Tribunal. He has permitted his fear of litigation against him to affect his representation of you." It just never occurred to me that my own attorney would be capable of such deplorable tactics. Those inadequate to the task and the deceivers always try to crush the weak and the disabled. How else can they claim victory?

The decision of Referee Switt was predictably favorable for the writer. However, the other side appealed and the decision was reversed inasmuch as the first hearing controls the second hearing.

In his brief to the second Master Arbitrator, Mr. Judas never included his errors, omissions or misrepresentations. Upon receipt of the adverse decision, he advised me that he could not appeal the decision of the second Master Arbitrator because "Jean Lorcheck of the American Arbitration Association decided your case has no merit." Apparently he was not aware that I had had conversations with Jean Lorcheck who was a supervisor at my insurance carrier. Mr. Judas had a duty and responsibility to submit the award to the Supreme Court for judgment but when it became apparent that he was not going to pursue this matter, I directed a legal stenographer to submit the award.

I instructed Mr. Judas to appeal, and he advised me that he was not an appeal's lawyer, that I should retain other counsel. Again, again and again, I attempted to retain counsel, times too numerous to mention, but my efforts were to no avail. It came to my attention again, again and again that my attorney, Mr. Judas was informing every attorney I attempted to retain that my case had no merit and that I was receiving psychiatric treatments, when he knew that was untrue. It was obvious the smear campaign by Mr. Judas was designed to injure and discredit me. I refused to be dominated by his malice. It is self-evident that the essential element of deception is humiliation. I was aware that my attorney, the deceiver, was desperately attempting to destroy my self-respect by humiliating and dehumanizing me and placing in public view that which he knew was an untruth. But we, the public, must refuse to be humiliated and dehumanized by those whose conscience can only be branded as deceptive; we must refuse to be crushed under the weight of their deceptions.

I was emotionally fragile and suffering constant, indescribable torturous head pains and severe pains throughout my body. I was also experiencing extreme weakness to extreme exhaustion to collapse, and the debilitating effects of sleeplessness were tearing me apart; it was so intense, so constant and so torturous that I "almost died." My torture went beyond all human endurance; I felt like I was bolted into a torture chamber. I realize that I cannot expect you to share my bitter agony unless you have had a similar experience, but I do expect you to share my deep feelings of concern for those innocents who will come after me.

Following many, many adjournments of the Examination Before Trial regarding my accident case, Mr. Judas' secretary advised me that the attorney for the other side wanted an adjournment. I called the other attorney to inform him that I do not agree with an adjournment, and the secretary informed me, "We did not want the adjournment; your lawyer did." Mr. Judas' secretary, "Mona," became belligerent and sarcastically asked, "Are you taking valium yet?"

In September of 1983, there was an order for an in-camera inspection of my full office medical records, and in December of 1983, I called the judge's chambers and inquired of the law secretary as to when a decision would be rendered. I was then informed that the judge never received the records. A member of my family contacted the record room, and it was discovered that they had been lost. Mr. Judas never inquired as to what the problem was.

Hopefully the rest of this saga will stimulate your disgust for the legal profession. Can we attempt to avoid becoming the victim of legal oppression when lawyers capitalize on the oppressed? I will allow you to be the impartial judge.

I needed an attorney for the appeal of the second Master Arbitrator's decision. There was a time limit for the appeal, and I was aware of the consequences if I missed the deadline. I contacted my cousin/attorney, "Monte," to assist me in retaining counsel for the appeal due to the fact that Mr. Judas was continuously discouraging attorneys from handling my legal matter and it was impossible for me to remain on the telephone close to my bed for any length of time. He retained an attorney on Long Island, a Mr. Turncoat, who came to my home and stated he did not want to attack "Joseph" because "We don't want to antagonize him." Oh, oh!

Mr. Turncoat informed me that it took two weeks to dictate the appeal. However, it took him over a year from the last decision rendered by the Supreme Court Judge to submit the rough draft to me. (It later came to my attention that the time limit is six months.) Before the rough draft was submitted to me, I received a telephone call from a friend at the "enemy camp" that they had overheard a conversation between Mr. Turncoat, the appeal's lawyer, and my attorney, Mr. Judas. In words or substance, they were engineering a delay of the appeal hoping that I would, in the meantime, receive psychiatric treatments. In that event, Mr. Judas would then be blameless of his misrepresentation of me at the original Tribunal. I am sorry to have disappointed them!

The words *"sadistic cruelty"* are truly the only words that could describe their devious motives. By the procrastination of my appeal, Mr. Turncoat adversely affected my interests and caused needless anxiety. My confidence in his ability to represent me with any degree of integrity or confidence was completely destroyed. My attorneys just didn't care that they were taking advantage of the disabled. Up to this point I was unaware that my attorneys were capable of such a degree of malice. Their attitude was "Her body is destroyed; now let's try to destroy her mentally."

Numerous letters were sent to Mr. Turncoat (return registed receipt requested) on my behalf relating to the facts that must be included in the appeal. Mr. Turncoat forwarded the appeal to my home, went on vacation and left out all the facts that would have implicated my own attorney, Mr. Judas. I was advised by my cousin-Atorney that Mr. Turncoat was seeking to limit Mr. Judas' liability for legal malpractice. Enormous pressures were placed on me, and it was obvious that it was not a concern of Mr. Turncoat. Since lawyers have a similar mentality, the public must be made aware that this is the reason they find security in a conspiracy of deception. The insidious effects of their deceptions repelled me, and I felt helpless to attempt to stop Mr. Turncoat's attempts to cover Mr. Judas' gross errors. Due to their code of protective silence, my own attorneys were posing a continuing threat to justice. Lawyers continue to display an arrogant disregard for the rules of justice only because it is not recognized by our judicial system as an issue. It is for this reason that they maintain an over-inflated sense of being protected by our judicial system.

Is this revealingly representative of a mere handful of attorneys? The writer thinks not!

During the course of the proceedings, Mr. Judas instructed me not to mention my daily log since it would be detrimental to my case. At this point, I did not have a copy of the daily log in my possession and, in addition to my ever-present torturous pains, I now had an added frustration of what could be in that daily log that would be detrimental to my case. Mr. Turncoat informed me, "You are lucky you have "Joseph" as your lawyer; he knows there was an error in diagnosis." At that time I thought he meant the fact that Doctor Morsey was unable to diagnose the symptomology of violent allergenic reactions to medications.

My cousin-attorney "Monte" sent a letter to Mr. Turncoat stating, "I made the initial contact with your office on behalf of Ms. Sansiviero, who later retained you, in reliance upon your representation that you would have no reservations about calling into question the manner by which Lawyer Judas handled this case for Ms. Sansiviero."

When I became aware that Mr. Turncoat was refusing to include the misrepresentation of Mr. Judas, I threatened to pull my file and after much aggression, he reluctantly and begrudgingly included Mr. Judas' gross errors anywhere they would fit. Mr. Turncoat, being extremely distraught, then wrote a letter to me stating that he will not be responsible for the outcome. I discovered years later that the decision of the Original Tribunal was final with no right to appeal. Had I followed Mr. Turncoat's bad counseling, there would have been a question concerning Mr. Judas' misrepresentation at the original Tribunal.

Let me digress for a moment regarding a third attorney, Mr. Jeorgio, who was responsible for reinstating me in a *very small disability policy.* He kept inquiring: "Are you receiving psychiatric treatments yet? Are you taking valium yet?" Please note neither valium nor anti-depressants were ever prescribed by any physician or neurologist. I was aware that Mr. Jeorgio and Mr. Judas were close friends and that they were waiting for me to begin receiving psychiatric treatments. I was advised by a paralegal that Mr. Jeorgio was delaying the doctor's examination for his own gain, so from the telephone next to my sickbed I contacted the insurance company and the examination was scheduled.

My. Jeorgio, apparently very angry, slammed the telephone down and proceeded to advise me in writing, "I must insist you cease calling or contacting the insurance company representatives." I was reduced to invalid status, with absolutely no income and he was angry because of my interference.

When I was reinstated, Mr. Jeorgio informed me, "This is what I am entitled to." I signed an agreement for one-third of recovery plus twenty percent of future recovery of my monthly disability checks.

Mr. Turncoat inquired as to the amount of money paid to Mr. Jeorgio. When he learned of the monies being sent to Mr. Jeorgio from my monthly disability checks, he exclaimed loudly, "What?" Due to the surprised tone of his voice, I inquired of an upcoming President of the Bar Association, for whom I always had a great deal of respect, whether it was ethical for Mr. Jeorgio to be receiving twenty percent of future recovery of my monthly disability checks. He said that Mr. Jeorgio wasn't doing anything wrong. I also made the same inquiry of a law secretary, Manning, who stated: "He wasn't doing anything wrong."

My sister Margaret requested my permission to write a letter to the Bar Association on my behalf, but I advised her not to waste her time. Nevertheless, she wrote the letter, and the Bar Association advised her in December of 1985: "After deliberation, the committee determined that there was no breach of the code of professional responsibility on the part of the attorney. The determination of the committee does not preclude you from pursuing any legal remedy which may be available to you."

What is conspicuous to the public is the fact that we are hampered by the very legal structure that was designed to protect us. A new legal discipline must be created when an upcoming President of the Bar Association, Mr. Toro, and a law secretary, Manning, agree that Mr. Jeorgio wasn't doing anything wrong, although numerous others within the judicial system agreed that it was unethical. I was patronized. Has the Bar Association, by their very inaction, proven that the disciplinary process in New York State is inaccessible to the public? The process is available to the public, but it only works in favor of the lawyer. Our system uses the law to protect themselves, thereby polluting the ethic's process. Since our system manipulates and presents it to us as law to their own advantage, authority ceases to exist. It is a crucial insight into the structure of a legal system. It is ironic that we, the public, expect justice from a court-run panel of lawyers exclusively chosen to monitor correct principles of conduct, better known as ethical considerations, who are part of the country club/Bar Association clan.

To the writer, it is akin to the manner of justice discharged in a foreign country that we sanction for denying human rights. Let us open our eyes to this judicial flaw that allows chaos and confusion to endure.

The Bar Association, or Grievance Committee, was established to protect the public from lawyers who are deficient in moral strength, but when the Bar Association distances itself from that which they know to be truth and facts, disregarding our legitimate complaints as unworthy, there is absolutely no opportunity to alter one's principles or actions. The issue is not whether there is insufficient openness of judicial proceedings to protect the public; the public *"knows"* there is insufficient openness. Due to the present lack of openness, the Bar Association has been ineffectual in controlling illegal activities. They are currently engaged in a legal process that allows, by silent consent, the door to open to even greater deceptions and increased professional misconduct. This is a legitimate public issue that must be addressed by the policy makers. By the inaction of the Bar Association, they automatically authorized my attorney to deceive me without fear of any disciplinary action. Consequently, lawyers have the power to control and manipulate the public. This is the unmistakable message that the Association is giving to attorneys: "There are no boundaries," a carte blanche to do whatever they wish. We, the public, are susceptible to the deceptions of any lawyer because of the Bar Fraternity unity, which is ample evidence for the need for reform.

Returning again to the appeal, Mr. Turncoat had altered the wording relating to monies that were sent on my behalf to Mr. Jeorgio to an untruth that monies were sent "by the insurance company." I advised Mr. Turncoat that my sister Margaret had made a copy of the changes and, therefore, please correct the altered changes to reflect the truth. When it became apparent that he was not going to make the corrections, my sister Margaret went to the Appellate Division in Brooklyn (quite a distance) to make the necessary corrections.

After learning that the corrections had been made, Mr. Turncoat became very aggressive and offensively nasty and then wrote: "I told you I would make the necessary corrections. There is no cause for your constant pressure. It was coincidental I called Mr. Turncoat's office on another matter, and "Merrol," his secretary, advised me: "Mr. Turncoat just dictated the letter today," which was "February 3, 1984." He had dictated the letter to the Appellate Division, correcting the error, and predated the letter "February 1, 1984," all in an attempt to hide unethical behavior.

FLAGRANTE DELICTO! *(Caught in the act)*

Mr. Turncoat showed little regard for the unspeakable emotional stress and strain that he was placing on me while I was reduced to invalid status. He was only concerned with his attempt to conceal the unethical behavior of Mr. Jeorgio.

I sent three witnesses to the Appellate Division, then in session in Nassau County, to ascertain if Mr. Turncoat would present the facts surrounding the misrepresentation of Mr. Judas at the Original Tribunal. They informed me that at no time during his oral argument did he refer to these facts nor did he even mention his name. One of the witnesses had reproached Mr. Turncoat for not presenting the fact that Mr. Judas had erroneously stated at the H.S.A. Panel Hearing that the plaintiff was receiving psychiatric treatments when she was never at any time treated under said specialty. I was informed that Mr. Turncoat's face became flushed, and he quickly dismissed the complaint with the statement that the correction was included under misconduct.

I was paying $10,000.00 *(of borrowed monies)* to Appeal's Attorney Turncoat, who was making every effort to protect Mr. Judas from embarrassment, the attorney who had made the error. He was also attempting to limit my ability to sue him for legal malpractice. Paradox piled upon irony!

There are no penalties for these violations. Unfortunately this is the type of misconduct attorneys are capable of which goes far beyond description, and they have the audacity to hide behind the smug mask of respectability. My attorney's actions were the height of cruelty, contemptuous and wholly dispassionate. Wishing to be rescued from my own humanness, as Author Alan Leo said so well, I prayed that all the antagonistic forces of my lower self would not rise up and swamp me, knowing through my inner prompting that that, in itself, would cause me to become lower than those I considered to be my arch-enemies. Remember, if they betrayed me, they will betray you.

I have just begun to illustrate how well my attorneys have mastered the discipline of deception. I want to give you a heightened awareness of a situation that could ultimately affect you and your family.

An adverse decision was rendered against me both by the Appellate Division and the Court of Appeals inasmuch as the decision of the Original Tribunal was binding with no right to appeal. My attorney, Mr. Judas, now had to answer the Partial Summary Judgment. He attempted to submit an 'Answer' that could mislead the court into believing I was receiving psychiatric treatments, essentially because he did not want to admit to his misrepresentation of me at the Original Tribunal. I refused to sign. Thereafter, he screamed in a loud, biting and cutting manner, "When Turncoat, Jeorgio and I get through with you, we are going to make mincemeat out of you." I advised him, "If you don't admit to the truth, I will call CBS and NBC," and within forty-eight hours Mr. Judas applied to the Supreme Court to withdraw from my legal matter. The Supreme Court Judge first allowed him to withdraw stating, *"In the light of the obviously acrimonious feelings of the plaintiff…."* Thereafter, I dictated a letter to the judge through a legal stenographer explaining that *"Facts were grossly distorted. You have given license to Lawyer Judas to go forth and do the same thing to some other unsuspecting client."* The judge instructed him to remain as my attorney. He then appealed to the Appellate Division and made false statements of material fact: "Because of acrimony, strained relationship, severe differences," but, of course, Mr. Judas did not indicate that he was the cause of the acrimony. He stated in his legal papers: "She and I disagree as to what took place at the H.S.A. Hearing."

I encountered a great deal of resistance; the challenge appeared to be insurmountable. I was fragile and ill-equipped to meet the overwhelming pressures and demands of dictating. While racked on the bed of purgatorial tortures, as legal stenographers read the legal file to me, I slowly dictated and "again" included the fact that Mr. Judas had discouraged lawyers from handling my legal matter, in addition to the fact that Mr. Jeorgio stole monies from my disability checks. In Simon's New York Code of Professional Responsibility: *"In litigation, therefore, it is sufficient to report serious misconduct*

to the court which the action is pending."
The Appellate Division and the Court of
Appeals allowed Mr. Judas to withdraw due to
irreconcilable differences, although they were
well aware of his professional misconduct of
discouraging attorneys from handling my legal
matter. A fair and careful inquiry would have
established the truth regarding my attorneys,
which was the solemn responsibility of our
judicial system. Mr. Judas excessively used
and abused the system; our judicial system
did "nothing," the implications are ominous.
We, the public, are being legally crippled by
our own judicial system that has taken on
the appearance of justice. The courts were
insensitive to the truth; they were amoral.
Even though our court system has unlimited
investigative power, they did absolutely
nothing. This is a troublesome point for the
public when laws are conveniently ignored by

the highest levels of law enforcement for the benefit of lawyers. This continuous breach of law must be surgically removed.

By their inaction and disturbing silence, they lost sight of their own responsibility and deepened the legal chaos. They increased the already enormous room for abuse and fueled the inferno of injustice. I experienced the total absence of judicial support; their inaction can never be justified. The court itself by remaining passive and submissive in light of the facts empowered my lawyer to conduct himself in an unrelenting cycle of professional misconduct and excessive misuse and abuse of the legal process. By their inaction and open tolerance, they validated professional disreputable acts and permitted the improper handling of my case to continue. They allowed me to continue to wrestle with deception, which placed me at a tremendous disadvantage. The law was not faithfully executed in my case; consequently, my case is a direct reflection of a very deep destructive process in our judicial system regarding professional misconduct which we must view as an act of judicial violence against the public. This is a very dangerous threat to the public. By doing nothing, they not only permit increased professional misconduct, they promote it.

In a December of 1984 letter from Mr. Turncoat, he advised me that Mr. Judas would waive his fee if I settled the case; I refused. Eventually in 1996, just immediately prior to the time of trial, in the face of mounting evidence and the essential failure of his tactics, Mr. Judas admitted to liability; *he conceded defeat*. Our judicial system allowed Mr. Judas to play games with the system.

In Simon's Code of Professional Responsibility, "A lawyer who makes inadequate disclosures or uses improper threats to get out of a case may later face a grievance committee...." Mr. Judas never had to face a grievance committee. The word *"may"* should be eliminated and replaced with *"will,"* thereby removing 90% of imposing collisions between allegations and denials.

I have personally witnessed a relaxed tolerance and indifference to professional misconduct within our judicial system, which official disorder raises disturbing issues. Illegal acts continue to greatly multiply and flourish; our judicial system has exhausted the public's patience. The courts are using taxpayers' money to permit attorneys to abuse the system, a costly failure with an immense price to the public. This is a very dangerous attitude on the part of our judicial system and a serious legal issue of judicial integrity. This case brings into sharp focus that our judicial system does not provide protection for the victim; they have little interest in acting decisively in cases of professional misconduct in the absence of prejudicial publicity. If we do not solve this shameful problem of injustice, you and your family may very well be suffocated by the very system we expect will protect us. This situation of deception and denial must be confronted and defeated. This ongoing scandal is a classic example of display of arrogant abuse of power by my attorneys and the judicial system, both of whom have assumed more power and authority than is rightly theirs, which presents an intriguing idea of justice.

We, the public, believe that impartiality is the basic theme of justice, so if we are going to have even a "hint" of justice, we must force our judicial system to change the fundamental nature of their thinking and rid themselves of their prejudices; their prejudiced decisions affect all of us.

My attorneys betrayed a trust and knowingly engaged in the violation of the law; there was not even a slight enforcement of the law by our judicial system. There is no question that the judicial system was completely aware that my attorneys were consciously making every attempt to victimize me. By their inaction, three elements were jeopardized: Violation of public trust, interference with the administration of justice and the judicial system itself not only became an active participant in the grinding wheels of injustice, but became the source of injustice. There is no question that they buried the truth and turned a deaf ear to what they knew was unjust. Our decision-making authority, better known as our judicial system, is assumed to promote the rule of law and be committed to the common good of society; they are committed to the common good of lawyers!

How can our judicial system occupy a position of influence and status if they are inactive regarding professional misconduct? Our judicial system, by continuing to protect lawyers, permits itself to be a feckless judicial structure. By sweeping ethical considerations under the rug, their inaction, disturbing silence and losing sight of their own responsibility, I was largely ignored.

I wish to excite public interest with the flames of justice to force change so you can protect yourself against weak justice of which I, myself, was a victim. I truly hope to ignite and generate a controversy that will reverberate throughout the public at large which simply cannot be ignored.

It is common knowledge around the courthouse that lawyers are fiercely protected by our judicial system. I will also give you firsthand knowledge of the grand masters of judicial evasion who have caused judicial distrust.

In the wake of my complaint, our inactive judicial system did not respond sharply; in fact, they did not respond at all. I was urgently begging to be rescued from the compromising influence of a transparent and devious situation, and I was informed not to expect even a mere admonition to my attorney, Mr. Judas, to cease his professional disreputable acts.

At the present time our judicial system arbitrarily chooses their own code of ethics, allowing them to excuse themselves from relevant standards of judicial conduct. They should not be permitted to have their own code of ethics; this is a violation of the process they have sworn to support. It is also insulting to the public's sensibilities and shows disrespect for the very law we are supposed to be governed by. Because the courts have refused to overcome their natural temptation of being sympathetic towards their Fellow Attorneys, they have become the active force of leading attorneys into an even deeper realm of lawlessness. This is a grave flaw in our judicial system when sympathy towards Fellow Lawyers continues to be the acceptable lubricant for protecting lawyers.

Our judicial system was very much aware of my lawyer's misconduct and approved such conduct by their inaction. I became a product of the inactive judicial process. With respect to that misconduct, our judicial system holds a preconceived irrational opinion that it is acceptable to form a judgment beforehand without thoughtful consideration of the pertinent facts, issues or arguments. Due to this prejudgment without adequate consideration, our judicial system has justly earned the reputation of being a system that simply does not practice justice without prejudice, and we are threatened by this judicial deterioration.

Favoritism of lawyers is the culture; this continues to characterize our judicial system to this day. By telling you my experience, I hope to raise profound questions about the ethical lapses of the Appellate Division and the Court of Appeals with regard to professional misconduct of attorneys.

Apparently our judicial system feels they have a commitment to protect lawyers. They largely ignored the litigant who was reduced to invalid status. Essentially this is the twisted message our judicial system is giving: *"when you complain about a lawyer in the absence of prejudicial publicity, you will not receive the benefit of protection you should be provided according to law."* Our judicial system is informing the public we must accept these offensive imperfections, which is out of sync and violates the very purpose of our judicial system. Bear in mind that *"ethics"* always deals with what you ought to do, apparently a perfect expression of their predisposed minds, which denotes a state of mind that interferes with fair judgment.

By their inaction, our judicial system allowed my attorneys to be exempt from the law; justice was the missing ingredient. The ironic twist is that the very law that was created to protect the public victimizes us. If we, the public, are unable to move from the shadow of injustice, we will continue to be exploited. How can we not be filled with suspicion? If we cannot depend on our judicial system for impartial, dispassionate decisions in our broken, chaotic world of social unrest, whom do we approach? No matter how justified our judicial system may feel they are, they are acting outside the limits of their judicial duties, resulting in invalid decisions and depriving the public of justice.

How can we, the public, expect justice from our judicial system when we have become the objects of injustice, simply because the system protects lawyers? When we make a formal accusation or complaint against a lawyer, our judicial system has assumed that automatically gives them permission to substitute their own judgment and act beyond the limits of the law, because they have been distracted from their very purpose. We, the public, must not minimize the disastrous consequences of this very serious issue of refusal of those who exercise authority to abide by the truth because it definitely affects *"us."*

Our judicial system does not require incompetent, deceptive attorneys to be accountable for their shortcomings. It is for this reason that we, the public, are exposed to calculated manipulation. The inaction of our judicial system regarding professional misconduct simply escalates the potential of injustice to an alarmingly higher level. When they fail us by protecting attorneys who are guilty of professional misconduct, it becomes a false system of law. This activity illustrates an even greater realization of the meaning of injustice.

Are we, the public, going to permit these offending forces to continue to be active within our judicial system? At the present time, the system fails to operate effectively because they do not act decisively against lawyers who have committed professional disreputable acts, and this perpetual barrier to justice is nothing more than <u>THE HURLING</u> of wholesale assaults against the public.

   The attitude in our judicial system is: *"If lawyers go beyond the legal boundaries set by the Code of Professional Responsibility, so what?"* Thereby creating an attorney's paradise. We, the public, are justified in raising this forceful alarm since we are disadvantaged by this apathetic inaction of our judicial system. This is the time for righteous indignation. To our judicial system, we say: *"Look in the mirror. Surely you know your inaction has a corrupting influence on your Fellow Lawyers who already have distain for the law, and we, the public, suffer. We remain defenseless due to the loss of your moral compass."*

   This is an extremely dangerous precedent that has been set over the years when there is unethical use of the public for one's own advantage or profit by lawyers who have no moral principles, and our judicial system does nothing. This discrimination must be halted now! By their inaction, the judicial system gives the public a clear message: *"You, the public, do not have a right to hold standards for those in authority. We refuse to bow to public pressure even if it is for the public's insatiable hunger for justice."*

Bear in mind, our inactive judicial system themselves have fostered this attitude on the part of the public. Can we even *"consider"* reducing impartial, dispassionate decisions within our present judicial system without public exposure? Not with the degree of decay that now exists in the minds of these so-called legal minds regarding professional misconduct. We must strongly voice our opposition to this conflict of thought already manifested within our judicial system in order to break the barrier of judicial silence, defrost their image and rid our system of excessive judicial secrecy. Only public exposure can eliminate these happenings.

A supposedly well-respected appeal's attorney on Long Island, Mr. Booma, stated in his undated (1995-1996) appeal to assist Mr. Judas to withdraw: *"It is strikingly clear that an attorney who has been subjected to such abuse by a client...."* Innocent though I was, Mr. Booma made the other person the issue; the victim became the perpetrator.

Mr. Booma continued: *"In the best interest of that client, when the relationship has become so lacerated and shaken, that attorney cannot continue to put forth his best efforts on behalf of the client."* "However, Mr. Booma never stated in his appeal that Mr. Judas was the cause of the relationship becoming lacerated and shaken because Lawyer Judas initiated the acrimonious situation. Again, the victim becomes the perpetrator!

Mr. Booma continues in his appeal: "After vilifying her attorney...." At Mr. Judas' Examination Before Trail, he answered the following question under oath:

Q. "Do you feel the plaintiff destroyed and lacerated your reputation?"

A. "My reputation? No."

Again, the victim becomes the perpetrator! The courts knew Mr. Judas engaged in conduct involving dishonesty, fraud, deceit and misrepresentation, yet the legal community remained silent, and this ongoing indifference was an additional complicating situation. We, the public, must draw the conclusion that our judicial system just does not care that incompetent and deceptive attorneys take advantage of the weak and disabled.

The judicial system has an awesome ethical responsibility, and they violate that ethical responsibility when they are inactive. The courts were advised that Mr. Jeorgio stole monies from my monthly disability checks; they were also informed of the misrepresentation and professional disreputable acts of Mr. Judas. Yet both lawyers did not even receive a mildly negative notice from the Appellate Division or the Court of Appeals. A casual examination of the evidence would have placed my attorneys in a highly questionable light; the evidence was clearly identifiable.

We, the public, must not have a charitable view of this insufferably hypocritical behavior. Since our judicial system did not seek the truth, it became an exercise in futility for me.

The ultimate reality: It is not what action our judicial system takes that causes gut-wrenching grief and suffering beyond measure to the public, but what action they constantly fail to take with regard to professional misconduct. This misconduct unleashes a wave of injustice against the public allowing us to be swept into the muddy waters of injustice. Their inaction embraces blindness to reality allowing lawyers to be above the rule of the law.

We, the public, can and must make it impossible for our judicial system to continue to inflict their illegal variety of the administration of the law for the benefit of their Fellow Attorneys. Public exposure will significantly affect whether they will be tempted to enforce this mask of disgrace to the point that we allow our judicial system to exercise their own brand of justice regarding professional misconduct, to that point are we resistant to justice.

Again and again, I attempted to retain counsel for my legal matter and again and again, Mr. Judas opposed my efforts and advised every attorney that my case had no merit, that I was receiving psychiatric treatments; he was well aware that I was never at any time treated under said specialty.

By his professional disreputable acts, Mr. Judas was making certain that I would not have the effective assistance of counsel, a continuing episode of which our judicial system was very much aware. Surely our judicial system realized their inaction has a significant demoralizing effect on the public, and their prejudiced, dispassionate decisions are a contributor to injustice, thereby pronouncing judicial sentence against themselves. Our judicial system has depreciated, cheapened and weakened their own authority.

I was now confronting the most tremendous obstacle an individual has to cope with -- betrayal. I found myself in a decidedly evil situation because of the inescapable message our judicial system was sending me: *"We don't care that your lawyer, Mr. Judas, is discouraging attorneys from handling your legal matter while you are reduced to invalid status. We don't care that Mr. Jeorgio stole money from your monthly disability checks and, if lawyers go beyond the standards of behavior or overstep recognized boundaries, that is perfectly permissible. We are vigorously patting our Fellow Lawyers on the back and we have the power to continue it."*

Our judicial system just does not consider their failing to maintain professional responsibility a critical judicial deficiency. We, the public, must pronounce and proclaim that to be wholly unacceptable and contrary to law.

I was injured by a legal decision that infringed upon my legal rights. My case is an example of how deeply into chaos our judicial system is capable of plunging in the absence of public exposure. The absence of this exposure causes our judicial system to manipulate the law that was created to protect us.

Mr. Judas continued to discourage attorneys from representing me for many years (1981 to 1995), which attacked the vulnerable areas of my inner self. By his actions, it was Mr. Judas' intent to discredit, and quietly and deceptively suppress; his ability to utilize this flamboyant talent for professional misconduct was generated by our own inactive judicial system.

We are presently forced to accept the faults, frailties and imperfections of our judicial system due to the fact that their conduct is completely unregulated; this must be amputated. Something else must be substituted for a system that does not effectively protect the rights of clients. We are certainly not expecting more than our judicial system is required to give us under the law.

I trust these experiences will remain a shocking indictment of the great failure of our utterly deficient judicial system to protect the public's interests.

We, the public, must be willing to challenge that which we consider to be illegitimate. It must be dragged up from the bowels of the earth and exposed to public view. We must challenge the shameful behavior of authority figures, because by our failure to act, we are rendering injustice agreeable and surrendering to cynicism, and you could be that next victim. When our judicial system does not seek the truth that does not compel or constrain us to shrink from being critical of that which is unjust simply because it is the Appellate Division or the Court of Appeals. They have given themselves the right to release themselves from obligation for their own deficiencies, utter failures, omissions, neglect and falling short of their obligations; the inevitable consequence of this accursed cancer is injustice, similar to a current running opposite to the main flow of water or fuel that consumes its own engine. This common practice represents a major setback to justice; it is referred to as the judicial system that works for itself and its colleagues.

There are two fundamental thoughts to consider:

1. Either our judicial system does not comprehend the diabolical effects of their inactions, which is doubtful...

Or

2. They do comprehend the diabolical effects of their inaction, but they are not concerned about it, which promotes cynicism.

Let us strike a more personal note as you continue to read this calendar of events. You must ask yourself this burning question: "Who will be the next victim of an attorney making blundering errors, being deceptive and undertake to conceal his incompetence? You can be confident that our paralyzed, narcissistic judicial system will violate their own law and employ the Biblical Pontius Pilate approach of washing their dirty hands and walk away from the truth." It is not impossible for the public to understand their motives, but their inaction is in direct opposition to the law they are supposed to defend and represent.

We, the public, refuse to continue to be the target of your inaction. We are paying billions of dollars a year to support a judicial system that behaves as a rubber stamp regarding professional misconduct; our judicial system is not designed as a rubber stamp. They constantly trample on our legal rights by functioning outside the law and approving professional misconduct as a matter of routine. The public lacks respect for the dignity of our judicial system regarding professional misconduct. The more we refuse to face this endemic problem, the worse it will become for us. We continually face this restriction of justice, and we must not feel we are powerless to stop it.

Our judicial system has proven they do not seek the truth regarding professional misconduct. Consequently, they have unavoidably made themselves part of the controversy and, in my plight, they have done just that.

This is, indeed, a thorny, hot-button issue that must be challenged because, obviously, our permissive judicial system has lost focus of what their responsibility is to the public. We do not want to be abused by an authority that does not serve the interest of the truth and the public. We must refuse to accept the chill of this corrupted atmosphere regarding professional misconduct. We must assert our will for justice and trust the outcries of the public for justice will be heard. Our legal system must not make attempts to quiet our legitimate criticism. We demand that a standard must be met. By constant public outcries, we will participate in the formation of a policy that will protect the public. We must resist the temptation that this is a systemic disease and we can do nothing about it, or that there are no remedies to this underlying problem. Dispel that myth immediately; this is not an uncorrectable disease. We must forcefully call upon the policy makers to initiate a resistance movement against professional misconduct to insure that these reforms become law -- we will accept nothing less! A new dimension is in order. We want to be protected. Reforms of this nature to eliminate negative powerful holds on the public are always painful but, trust me, it will not be as painful as the unspeakable deep wounds our present judicial system has knowingly inflicted on the public in the past by their willful blindness. This is an unpopular conflict in the legal profession which must be resolved immediately. Let us, the public, force policy makers to take the necessary steps to do that which they have not done in the past -- protect the public! Policy makers, you cannot afford to ignore the necessity of this reform.

I realize that we cannot legislate into existence unprejudiced legal minds regarding professional misconduct and, since our legal system is largely unwilling to police their own profession; it falls on us to pressure those in authority to expose the offenders to public scrutiny.

A Governor on the West Coast spoke out against "lawyer bashing" but, unfortunately, what the West Coast Governor failed to remember is, *"They deserve it."* Lawyers have achieved the public distinction of having a high-powered, uncommon aptitude for legal bacteria due to their unimaginable and limitless ability for deception. Should our judicial system be embarrassed because of their acceptance of excessive misuse and abuse of the system by attorneys while we are being deprived of our legal rights? Why should they be? They have the power! There are judges who were once lawyers who judge lawyers -- *such a comfortable arrangement!* It is because of this comfortable arrangement that lawyers can engage in whatever illegal activity they select without fear of censure, condemnation or reproach. Presently *"only highly egregious and highly publicized cases"* of professional misconduct are dealt with decisively. Why is our judicial system unable to accept this truth? Because it convicts them!

We, the public, can be confident when there is any illegal activity on the part of attorneys with the absence of prejudicial activity by subtle and refined methods, the Appellate Division exercises extreme care to deliberately overlook such activity; this, in itself, is an act of betrayal by the proud and mighty. This is an inappropriate position that they have assumed, which is a demonstration of contempt of decent citizens seeking justice. We must come to grips with this harsh reality. No doubt our judicial system will attempt to engage in self-justification and defend their position by whatever outward action they select in disparagement of this criticism, but without our criticism the system will continue to be shortsighted and increasingly sympathetic towards their Fellow Lawyers.

We must refuse to allow predisposed legal minds to have this option. This is a troublesome point for the public; we must not give acceptance to the appearance of justice. Inaction can only be described as a formula for *"pretended justice"*. Unfortunately, they have a great advantage over us. We must limit the judicial system's capacity for *"pretended justice"* so they will literally be unable to render themselves ineffective or reduce their inactions to a state of injustice. This very common, unrecognizable inaction of the system exists on an alarming scale, and it reduces the unsuspecting public to the state of being totally insignificant. Due to this inaction, we fall victim to injustice which means the judicial system becomes the cause of contradiction, setting a trap for the public which, through no fault of its own, is ignorant of the invisible trap. They must shoulder the responsibility of supplying the sword of injustice leading to the oppression of the public, which raises serious constitutional violations. This is such a great risk to the public; therefore, a detergent-type cleaning process must take place if there is to be any degree of transformation. What is the solution or cleansing process to avoid the future laceration of the public by judicial egoism? A dramatic reshaping or a profound shift will not occur until every state in the United States adopts a policy similar to the policy that has been adopted by thirty-seven other states. According to information received from the American Bar Association, dated February 26, 1999, all formal disciplinary complaints of lawyers must be made "public." Until this policy becomes mandated throughout the United States can we even consider resisting injustice; this is the only societal legal safeguard or defense that exists for the public. This remedy will be a touchstone on the issue of public protection against professional misconduct. This significant change or creation of a new legal discipline can be implemented very easily in our legal system. It is the only effective judicial restraint that can eliminate profound consequences for the public. If this is not adopted, our judicial system will continue to be a breeding ground for injustice with regard to professional misconduct. Our policy makers will be denying the very basis of justice.

In order to protect ourselves, we must organize and be the vital force for this much-needed change. Let us not wait in the wings to be invited. If we do, it will never happen; this initiative must move forward. It is common knowledge that reformers and whistleblowers are always purged and made the target of criticism, but however purged or criticized, there is no justification for doing *"nothing,"* and asks for an outpouring of community concern.

Since our inactive judicial system presently hides its failure, they will invariably be strongly opposed to any unpopular reforms, no doubt a course of action most difficult for them to accept. On the other hand, if these reforms do not become law, they will be informing the public they have no desire to purge the contaminated system so few of us hold in high esteem. The judicial system must not resist or challenge these reforms, which are the answer to the problems that retard justice. Since their resistance would be just another invitation to continue the corruption of truth, we must question their commitment to justice. If these reforms are not put into law, it indicates an inability on the part of our judicial system to bear contradiction or correction for the benefit of society. Unless these long overdue reforms take place in the very near future, the prospect for changing the attitude of our judicial system regarding professional misconduct is very bleak. Those who benefit and gain the most advantage are attorneys. We must recognize that the absence of these reforms will allow our judicial system to plummet even deeper into the domain of injustice, and we will continue to be left hanging on the horns of the dilemma called injustice. Additionally, there must be stronger penalties for violations. This would be the powerful means of persuading attorneys of doubtful integrity not to use and abuse the system.

We must admit our judicial system has been extremely successful in one particular area: They have protected their Fellow Lawyers with behind-the-scenes maneuverings and secret meetings, their "weakness," which scandalizes the public. It is a damaging trend which allows the Appellate Division to immunize themselves against dispassionate, questionable decisions. It is an elective privilege they should not have, because this option allows them to legitimize serious forms of injustice. We must lift the veil of secrecy to halt this judicial suicide. The high cost of judicial secrecy is always injustice; they must not be allowed to poison the very purpose and essence of our judicial system due to the incredible risk.

We, the public, bear the risk of injustice, our largest legal headache, and they must be forced to render an accounting of prejudicial decisions. We do not want serious consideration; we demand action with full intent to protect us.

Policy makers, hear our united demand for this sweeping policy that will transform this widespread problem in our tainted system. This is a very realistic goal! A positive, essential, radical court reform of this nature would usher in a judicial system that attorneys would have a healthy fear of offending and could mark the dawning of a new era of respectability. As a result, our judicial system will no longer be intoxicated by their own power or an undeserved respectability. They would be forced to rise above their feelings of sympathy towards their Fellow Attorneys and committed to the justice they swore to defend. Our judicial system will command not only statewide respect, but national and international respect as well.

We, the public, are declaring to the policy makers of our beloved country: "*Before we attempt to dictate to another country regarding pervasive civil and human rights and abuses, we should make these necessary radical changes in our own judicial system. In that way we will establish a concrete expression of justice.*" Our judicial system will then have a stature that cannot be measured.

Where will we find someone who will reject the justice principle? We certainly won't find them amongst judges who were once lawyers, who remain unconcerned that they are provoking displeasure on the unsuspecting public because of their prejudiced minds. We want to be protected and since our judicial system does not protect us, we must intensify our efforts and utilize every available means to accomplish our purpose. We must vigorously contend any attempt to deceive the public, actions now existent in our judicial system.

William Ide, III, past President of the American Bar Association (1993/1994), wrote the following in the July 1994 issue of the ABA Journal: PRESIDENT'S MESSAGE, THE WILL TO MAKE A DIFFERENCE.

"I would say there can be no meaningful reform of the Justice System if it is left only to the lawyers and judges."

We are all very much aware that our courts have failed to protect us, so we must become a self-protecting society by insisting on public exposure for professional misconduct. By such exposure, they will no longer be able to exercise power unjustly regarding this misconduct.

Is public expectancy for justice unrealistic? *Absolutely not*! *We will triumph.*

These are the much-needed transformations that will be accomplished by public exposure, and they will no longer be able to persist in their guilty silence:

1) The elimination of self-promoting power.

2) They will be forced "not" to be seduced

or consumed by their own power and not be caught up by their own importance.

3) They will no longer be the legal hangman.

4) Behind the scenes maneuverings will be vastly reduced since they will be a model of restraint.

5) The greatest obstacles on the path towards justice, prejudice and dispassionate decisions, will be eliminated.

6) The Appellate Division's ability to descend to compromise with injustice will be eliminated.

7) They will no longer have the option to immunize themselves against questionable decisions. *(Indeed, an unpleasant prospect for our judicial system.)*

8) They will at least strive not to impose their own views regarding professional misconduct, keeping betrayal of civil justice to a bare minimum.

9) They will be unable to yield to the convenience of injustice due to their sympathy towards their Fellow Lawyers.

10) They will be forced to use an approach that does not violate our legal rights.

11) The necessary restraint on power for more suitable decisions will exist.

12) They no longer will be operating under the assumption that they may automatically substitute their own judgment and act outside the law with respect to professional misconduct.

13) The art of discerning truth will be practiced flawlessly.

14) The abuse and misuse of our legal system by lawyers at the public's expense will be greatly reduced.

15) Competence within the legal profession will be increased.

16) Their ability to be the devil's advocate will be greatly diminished.

17) They will be unable to elevate their questionable choices to the status of justice.

18) The overwhelming temptation to be sympathetic towards their Fellow Lawyers will be eliminated.

19) The issue of accountability will be resolved.

20) They no longer have the option of inviting lawyers to be indifferent to their network of lies.

21) Their ability to continue the manufacturing of the complex situation of professional misconduct will be eliminated.

22) Their silence will no longer become the seal of approval.

23) There will no longer be public mistrust with regard to the expression of power and authority.

24) To seek justice, the very purpose for which our judicial system was established, will be accomplished.

It's time, ladies and gentlemen, it's time! As long as policy makers refuse public exposure, professional misconduct shall remain.

Being responsible to authority and to the prescriptions of the law is an absolute must for civil society, and there is no justification for acting otherwise. But authority must always be mindful of their responsibility to those they solemnly swore to protect, *"the public."*

We, the public, must not be subordinate to injustice simply because the source of injustice is our judicial system. We must not wait patiently for the final chapter yet to be written on court reform. We must challenge the system and act NOW. Decent people must stand up and be counted.

In May of 1985, while still reduced to invalid status, I was ineligible to receive further disability payments from my "very small" personal policy and, therefore, I had absolutely no income. In October of 1985, I was forced to relinquish my home, which was mortgage-free at the time of my accident.

It is important to note that in May of 1987, Doctor Gram was killed in an automobile accident and soon thereafter his family moved to Tennessee, and my full office medical records were shipped with their possessions.

Despite the fact that Mr. Judas was allowed to withdraw from my legal matter, he nevertheless continued again and again to oppose my efforts to retain counsel to handle my appeal on the Partial Summary Judgment. Four judges on Long Island, aware that Mr. Judas was discouraging attorneys from handling my case, did absolutely nothing. Our judicial system by remaining inactive, literally gave my attorney permission to continue to be the deceiver. This conduct alone should be sufficient enough to view our judicial system with great skepticism. At a pre-trial conference in Suffolk County regarding the Partial Summary Judgment, Judge DiMartino inquired of me: *"When are you going to get a lawyer?"* I replied: *"When my lawyer, Mr. Judas, stops bad mouthing me."* The judge immediately ordered the conference be held in the Judge's Chambers. Since there was a courtroom full of attorneys present, how else could Judge DiMartino shelter the well-known Mr. Judas from any further humiliation and embarrassment? Once in the Judge's Chambers, he stated *"You're not going to get a lawyer to take your case."* This statement by a Supreme Court judge clearly defines the deteriorating judicial attitude and is a testimonial to the very fabric of the legal community's mentality. Destruction of this appalling attitude is imperative before we can experience justice on any level. Coincidentally, this individual eventually served as an Appellate Division judge. Nevertheless, after making this statement, he recommended a nearby college where Mr. Harvey, an attorney, was retained. After completely reading my files, Mr. Harvey said, "Your lawyer screwed you."

The Appellate Court decision was rendered against me, and I, myself, dictated to a legal stenographer a short appeal to the Court of Appeals. Their decision read: "Ordered that the said motion for leave to appeal be and the same is hereby dismissed upon the ground that the order sought to be appealed does not finally determine the action within the meaning of the constitution."

The Court was aware that my attorney was discouraging other attorneys from handling my legal matter. I asked Mr. Harvey if he would represent me, but he informed me that I should retain another attorney for this matter. I continued to seek an attorney, but Mr. Judas again and again discouraged them, informing them that my case had no merit and that I was receiving psychiatric treatments. Mr. Judas was very much aware that I was never at any time treated under said specialty, but it also came to my attention that Mr. Turncoat was also making disparaging remarks about me. Does this happen with frightening and numbing regularity or is this an isolated situation? You can be assured that this is not an isolated situation.

In order for my legal stenographer to commence litigation against Mr. Judas, I needed my complete legal file but Mr. Turncoat, my Appeal's attorney, refused to release the file because there was a lien on it. After his refusal, I submitted a request to a Supreme Court judge explaining the circumstances. I realized he was aware of my physical condition and the fact that I was also unable to retain counsel, but a letter from his law secretary stated: "You are respectfully advised that Justice St. Moore subscribes to a strict policy against directives in a litigated matter on the basis of a letter request. Any disputes that may exist between you and your attorney, or former attorney, if such be the case, are best resolved by means of amicable settlement or accepted formal procedure." Suddenly our judicial system subscribes to a *"strict policy."*

I continued in my quest to retain a legal malpractice attorney for my suit against Mr. Judas, but again and again he continued to discourage attorneys. In 1987 as a last resort, still confined to a bed in an invalid status, I initiated litigation against Mr. Judas, dictating to a legal stenographer, and fully aware that there was a time limit for the initiation of this lawsuit.

Remember, I had a limited legal file in my possession due to Mr. Turncoat's refusal to release my file.

My lawyers systematically violated the law and our judicial system remained silent. I had absolutely no damage-control due to our inactive judicial system.

In 1989, the insurance adjuster contacted me, offered me $50,000.00 for the accident, and stated: "We don't need a lawyer." Inasmuch as I was unable to retain counsel, I accepted the settlement provided they include in the release the following clause: "All claims of injuries, medical expenses and economic loss suffered by the plaintiff for the period February 22, 1980 to September 30, 1980." They agreed and all monies were disbursed to pay outstanding medical bills and Mr. Turncoat's fee. The complete legal file was finally in my possession.

I continued in my attempt to retain counsel but Mr. Judas also continued to discourage the attorneys. He persisted to make statements in reckless disregard of the truth that I was under psychiatric care, although he was aware of the following letter from Dr Gram in my file: "This is written in an effort to prevent any further misunderstandings," and continuing,

"Mary Sansiviero was treated for nutritional purposes <u>only</u>. She was <u>never</u> treated under the specialty of psychiatry, as she never evinced at any time since her arrival in this office, any psychiatric coloration down to the present day. To the contrary, she has shown herself to be a remarkably well-balanced woman, and with an impeccable short-term and long-term memory." Mr. Judas was continuing to oppose my efforts to retain counsel by slander.

"Slander: whenever a person is prevented by the slander from receiving that which would be otherwise conferred upon her." My attorney was preventing me from retaining counsel, and I was absolutely helpless to stop it due to the inaction of our judicial system. Isn't it unbelievable that this type of situation could occur in our day and age?

We have a right to expect more from our judicial system. By their inaction, another vital issue is raised: What kind of other illegal, unlawful conduct does our inactive judicial system allow?

As long as this high-level activity continues in our judicial system regarding professional misconduct, the effects will be disastrous because attorneys will be readily influenced to continue to be a menace to society, causing incalculable damages and consequences to civil society. The threat to the public is so enormous that we must be warned of these dangers; this great permissiveness by our judicial system is a constant threat to justice.

In 1989, Mr. Carrio, Attorney for Mr. Judas, requested numerous documents. Due to my continuing extreme weakness and torturous pains, with no one available to assist me, I had no alternative but to provide Mr. Carrio with all my many, many files.

Our judicial system should now raise their eyebrows in disbelief of the deadly effects and consequences of their inaction. If we do not express dissatisfaction to our policy makers, there will continue to be irreparable harm inflicted on the public. Since we previously have not been able to trust our judicial system with relation to professional misconduct, public exposure directed at the deficiencies in our judicial system will do that which the public conceives as impossible. We will ultimately have a judicial system that is incapable of deceit and dispense the law with unparalleled integrity. Let the public hear the evidence! Let the public know about passing the trash! Let publicity be a high-alert wake-up call for the decent people of our beloved State of New York and our beloved country.

Since the courts have shrunk from their responsibility, having failed to fulfill their fundamental responsibilities of protecting the public, we must exert pressure, influence and force and continue to "fight" for this vital change. We must speak out courageously to defend justice in an effort to cleanse this earthquake of judicial disorder. Let us spark a debate regarding professional misconduct that can never be silenced. We can do it!

What expectations can we possibly have regarding behavior patterns in our streets, schools and universities if what most of us regard as our most respected institution is inactive? A most unsettling reality to devote thought to is the fact that the decline of any society always has its origins within the most respected institutions. We must be vocal critics; we must continuously and forcefully speak out against the evils in our judicial system and if we do not, there will never be a structure of justice that will protect you and your family from unscrupulous lawyers and other injustices.

Our legal system bears resemblance to a person suffering from a massive infection or epidemic disease. We all witness this person dying, but we never make any attempt to attack the infection or disease. If we fail to do our part to literally attack this ongoing massive infection of inaction within our judicial system, there will continue to be a further declining slope of legal standards that will ultimately affect you and your family. It is absolutely fatal for us to be indifferent to this crucial situation; we have a moral obligation to fight injustice. There must be one steadfast purpose in our efforts, and that is to promote awareness for the sole purpose of protecting the public.

By public exposure we can generate reforms that will reach the absolute standard of excellence, reforms that will force our judicial system to be absolutely impartial with regard to professional misconduct. The task of reviving the eroded confidence in our judicial system will be an easy one. If public exposure is needed for this much-needed change, fine, but change there must be. We must band together under the banner of justice for a change that we cannot afford to ignore.

Although Mr. Judas continued to oppose my efforts to retain counsel for the legal malpractice suit, even in my indescribable torture, I persisted in my quest for counsel, which included attorneys in Suffolk, Nassau and Queens Counties, New York City, Upper New York and New Jersey. I even contacted the Cardinal's office in New York and was informed that they could not become involved. I dictated a letter to the Governor in October of 1987 informing him of my attorney's actions, and

I received the following response: "Our Constitution provides for the separation of the executive and judicial function of government. The Governor, therefore, is precluded from intervention in any judicial matter. Additionally, I must inform you that it is not the policy of our office to provide legal advice or assistance in individual or private matters. Signed: Counsel to the Governor."

Our judicial system should "again" raise their eyebrows in disbelief regarding the effects and consequences of their inaction. Surely our system is not without knowledge of the risk to the public.

By early October 1989, the following medical conditions had subsided: Hypperreflexia, cerebella ataxia, reverberating, wiggling posture, the widening of my eyes, diarrhea, disjointed ankles, sciatica in both legs, leaky bladder, mounds on upper chest and cyanotic condition. That same year I appeared at an Examination Before Trial *without the benefit of counsel.* I was still exhibiting involuntary movements, imbalance, suffering agonizing head pains, and pains throughout my body, together with extreme weakness to extreme exhaustion to near collapse. During the E.B.T. due to my obvious involuntary movements, a short recess occurred before questioning was resumed.

Upon returning home from the E.B.T., I was unable to rise from the wheelchair without the assistance of two persons and thereafter unable to rise from the bed for months to care for my personal needs.

During a brief "Discussion off the record" at the E.B.T. regarding Mr. Judas' professional misconduct of discouraging attorneys from handling my case, Mr. Carrio in a low tone stated: "He said he would not say anything more." This was now my third mistake. I believed

Mr. Carrio, the attorney for Mr. Judas. Despite Mr. Judas' prior numerous attempts to discredit and undermine me by discouraging attorneys from handling my case, I again attempted to retain counsel through a female friend who was a legal stenographer. Mr. Murray, her former boss, stated that Mr. Judas had informed him that "She was off the wall." When I contacted Mr. Murray regarding this statement, he replied: "I don't remember. Joseph is a friend of mine."

I desperately needed an attorney. What my three lawyers perpetrated against me during my invalid status together with the inaction of our judicial system brings a new meaning to the word "injustice."

At a Pre-Trial Conference in Nassau County before a Supreme Court Judge, I complained that Mr. Judas was discouraging attorneys from handling my legal matter. The judge inquired, *"Do you want to withdraw?"* And I replied, *"I will not.*" Yet that judge did not order Mr. Judas to cease his professional disreputable acts or even admonish him for his professional misconduct, but instead ordered that an E.B.T. be held, *knowing I was without the benefit or assistance of counsel.*

At a subsequent Pre-Trial conference, I requested a *Hush Order,* but Law Secretary Manning response was, *"No."* I then inquired, *"Are you going to direct Lawyer Judas to stop bad-mouthing me?"* And his reply was, *"No, he is protected by the First Amendment."* This very statement speaks volumes to the vulnerable public of the indifference that lay hidden beneath their judicial exterior. This inaction reinforced his behavior and further complicated my situation. This absence of action creates situation ethics, absolute ethics for the public and absolutely no ethics for lawyers.

In 1995, expert witness, Mr. Raymond, Professor of Law at the University School of Law, who is a member of the Ethic's Committee on Long Island and New York, stated: *"That is not so."* This is another version of existent conditions within our judicial system, which can only be characterized as uneven scales in the "old-boy" network. *This is not approaching chaos; this is chaos.* It is a situation that calls to mind ever so sharply the lack of professional conscience within our judicial system, rubbing salt in the already open wound.

Law Secretary Manning allowed Mr. Judas to hide behind the First Amendment, which is designed to be a defensive armor against injustice. Is this not a sign of judicial decline? My confidence in our judicial system was perpetually being destroyed because of the lack of support from those in authority.

Mr. Judas was guilty of aggravated harassment towards one who was reduced to invalid status. He lied in all the legal papers, was guilty of deceit with intent to deceive the court, and committed perjury throughout the Examinations Before Trial. Testimony was repeatedly inconsistent and contradictory, an outrageous misuse of the legal process. Yet our judicial system did not demand perjury charges, especially when the perjury was very evident. Consequently, there was a blend of arrogance and incompetence in our legal system. This fact is a sober reminder of just how capable our judicial system is of closing itself to justice. Judicial intervention was sought and denied. Inaction always violates the very core of our judicial system.

Unless changes take place in our judicial system, attorneys will continue to practice within a legal structure that gives them "license" to do as they wish against the public. Professional conduct is a matter of ethics between lawyers and not between lawyers, and clients.

Why does the apathy of our judicial system manifest a character of the lowest tone? Because they are apparently unable to grasp the complexities of their own prejudicial minds and their little sense of what justice really is. By definition, judges should possess the knowledge of what justice is.

Our judicial system has definitely without question protected attorneys. When they do so, they violate the very standards of judicial practice that they have sworn to uphold. Why is this situation very critical? Because they are responsible only to themselves.

The attorney for Mr. Judas' carrier, Mr. Carrio, would not return phone calls nor would he respond to letters. When I inquired when Mr. Judas would be available to testify, Mr. Carrio's answer was: "What do you want me to do, grab him by the scruff of the neck and have him come in and testify?" Finally at a Pre-Trial Conference in 1990, the judge ordered Mr. Carrio to go downstairs in the courthouse where Mr. Judas was always present. It was thereafter agreed on a date for Mr. Judas to appear and testify. While waiting for their answer, the judge stated to me, "So, you are the one who doesn't like lawyers." Again, the victim becomes the perpetrator. Bear in mind that I was still experiencing agonizing torturous pain and was near collapse from extreme weakness to extreme exhaustion. It continued to be "necessary" when traveling to lie down on the backseat of the automobile; I would fall asleep while waiting for my legal matter to be called. Previous to

Mr. Judas'E.B.T my involuntary movements had completely subsided.

I later requested legal stenographers to read aloud the many files that were in my possession, and I then dictated questions that were enlarged to such an extent that one could read them easily from several feet away. When I made the attempt to read small print, I would literally be unable to speak and the torturous pains and extreme exhaustion increased.

Prior to the EBT of Mr. Judas and upon my requesting a Referee be present at Mr. Judas' EBT, Law Secretary Manning's responded *"No, our judicial System does not have sufficient funds for that"*.

Mr. Judas continuously and excessively used and abused our Judicial System due to his reckless disregard for the truth using taxpayers' money, but "once again" I was ignored.

In 1990, at the E.B.T. of Mr. Judas, Mr. Carrio posed an objection in ninety-nine of the one hundred questions in a very strong attempt to frustrate the examination. To add to my already impossible situation, I was now faced with an incompetent attorney, Mr. Carrio, who did not know that Mr. Judas could be examined as an expert witness. When the examination was finished, I was unable to speak and unable to get out of the wheelchair without the assistance of two other individuals. Thereafter, I was unable to rise from the bed for months to care for my personal needs, even with the help of two people.

Following the submission of the transcripts to the court in December of 1992, at a Pre-Trial Conference, Law Secretary Manning stated: "There are continuous objections to proper questions. Do everyone a favor, and get another lawyer in there". This was the first "hint" of judicial assistance I observed.

Another E.B.T. was ordered. Mr. Judas' attorney, Mr. Carrio screamed over the telephone in a very loud and aggressive manner, "They don't have the right to order me off your case." He was apparently very agitated! My case should have been submitted to the Grievance Committee due to the frustration of the E.B.T., but no such action was taken. I had asked the Law Secretary Manning, "who is going to pay for the Examination Before Trial?" and the response was, "You are." The law secretary knew I was indigent, yet I had to pay for another person's errors. How unresponsive our judicial system is to the poor; the law is not equally applied to the poor. There is no justice for the economically deprived; privileges for the poor are rarely enforced. I personally experienced this pressure due to the inactive judicial system.

In 1992, as I attempted to rise from the bed, the room would not stop spinning and I collapsed to the floor, was taken to the hospital by ambulance, and diagnosed with a bone fracture and multiple bruises.

In March of 1993, at an E.B.T., Mr. Judas was asked the following question:

Q. "Were you aware at the time of the H.S.A. Panel Hearing that plaintiff was never at any time treated under the specialty of psychiatry?

A. "I was aware at the time that Doctor Gram did have some specialty in that area with nutrition."

Law Secretary Manning's ruling was that the response to the last question was sufficient. There was no question in my mind that the ruling was completely erroneous, but I had no choice but to accept it.

However, in January of 1993, at the Examination Before Trial, I *"knew"* I already had an acceptable answer:

Q. "I am going to ask you again: Are you aware that the plaintiff was never at any time treated under said specialty?

A. "I am not aware of that."

I was thereafter able to tolerate Law Secretary Manning's absolutely incompetent ruling. Furthermore, law secretaries should not be rendering decisions that Supreme Court Judges are being paid to render.

Protection of attorneys continues to be a dominant force in the courts, making it increasingly difficult for the public to experience justice. I trust this accounting of events will cause the adrenalin to rush through the veins of those involved. We, the public, are trapped in an institution that clings to the adage: *"Protect our lawyers at any cost and if you are betrayed, so what!"*

Due to the judicial willingness to generally ignore that which is *"just"* regarding professional misconduct, equal protection and due process no longer exist for us. I went through the established channels, and the judicial system did what was convenient, *"They conveniently turned their heads."* Due to their inaction in the area of professional misconduct, they have made themselves unworthy of respect, and allowed themselves to become the greatest hypocrisy in modern times. Ultimately, the public becomes the victim of the enormous grief from the wounds of that shameful hypocrisy.

During a Pre-Trial Conference, Law Secretary Manning stated sarcastically: "I am going to dismiss this case." This statement was made at the time that I had been reduced to invalid status while suffering agonizing pain for sixteen years. I was now fully aware that I could not expect justice from my own judicial system.

In addition, Law Secretary Manning remarked as he flipped through papers, *"You are a bulldog,"* and I answered, *"I didn't want to handle this case."* He then directed that a number of questions that were objected to at the E.B.T. should be answered, and Mr. Carrio, the attorney for the insurance company, submitted a notarized supplement to Mr. Judas' deposition which was to be deemed part of the January, 1993 testimony. Mr. Carrio was providing answers of "I don't know" as to whether certain medical reports were submitted to the Original Tribunal, knowing the decision of the original Tribunal contained a listing of medical reports submitted. I telephoned Law

Secretary Manning and asked: "Isn't he supposed to answer those questions," and the Law Secretary's response was: "He's supposed to." The judicial system did not play a forceful role in my legal matter.

My niece, Karen from Westchester County, returned to Long Island again to write numerous letters requesting answers to questions that were not submitted initially according to Court Order.

At the end of 1994, Mr. Carrio inquired if I wanted to settle, and I responded, "Yes." Mr. Carrio then suggested that we start at $500,000.00. I was still unable to retain counsel to represent me in this matter due to Mr. Judas' discouraging remarks to other attorneys, and the amount of settlement was withdrawn. Due to the inaction of our judicial system, I continued my legal matter without the benefit of effective legal assistance.

In 1995, there was an unexpected turn of events. I contacted Mr. Farina, a well-respected negligence attorney on Long Island, and explained my need for expert witnesses. He highly recommended Mr. Sans of East Norwich, New York, who had expertise in the no-fault field, and he was retained in an effort to determine if the Original Tribunal was handled properly. I now realized the pleasures of conducting business with a "competent and honest" attorney. After reviewing the files, Mr. Sans stated: "Your lawyer shafted you." In his legal memorandum, he included the following conclusions: "Attorney exercised extremely poor judgment. It was bad representation on the part of the attorney."

Mr. Carrio, attorney for Mr. Judas, was now pressing for the names of any expert witnesses. Inasmuch as Mr. Judas was still discouraging attorneys from handling my case, I was deeply concerned and in June of 1995, I wrote to the Administrative Judge as to whether I was obliged, under the circumstances, to submit the names of expert witnesses. The law secretary for the Administrative Judge responded: "Please be advised I am precluded from rendering legal advice to litigants." Although the judge was aware of Mr. Judas' disreputable acts, he did absolutely nothing! By the very inaction of our judicial system, they have broken their trust with the public. In our courts, the client is irrelevant.

My legal secretary proceeded to type summonses for every physician, chiropractor and therapist who had treated me, but Law Secretary Manning, knowing I was unable to retain counsel because of Mr. Judas' professional misconduct, stated loudly and aggressively, *"You are abusing the system."* Isn't it interesting, he did not state that *"Mr. Judas was abusing the system,"* but that I was abusing the system? The message received from this statement led me to believe that I did not have the right to defend myself. Again, the victim becomes the perpetrator!

During a conference before a retired Supreme Court Judge, Mr. Carrio, attorney for Mr. Judas, offered $50,000.00, and the judge informed me that I could not receive any more than that because I had signed the release and settled the no-fault case for $50,000.00. The trial attorney whom I had eventually retained informed me: "That is not true."

The judicial system, sworn to serve us, only grieved me. Although this judge is one of the most respected judges on Long Island, I received his message loud and clear: "We want to get rid of you in the worst way, and we don't care how we accomplish it." When I refused the $50,000.00 Settlement, the judge became very hostile and abusive; I was extruded

by our legal system due to their lack of
zeal and commitment. If our judicial system
is capable of behaving in this manner to an
individual reduced to invalid status for over
nineteen years with torturous and agonizing
pain, what could that system be capable of
doing to you?

We were asked to wait in a room called the
"Trial Assignment Part," for our case to be
called. There were many lawyers present and
when the individual proceeded to call the
names of the legal matters to be heard next,
my last name was called, but never at any time
was the name of the attorney, Mr. Judas, ever
mentioned and he was the subject of my lawsuit.
I was later advised that this was again
another attempt to shelter Mr. Judas from any
embarrassment. I am not conveying these events
which you might view as a narrow spectrum, but
I wish to reveal a very severely contaminated

judicial system with regard to professional misconduct.

In 1990, during a Pre-Trial Conference, the Supreme Court Judge agreed to allow a physician from the insurance company to examine me, but Mr. Carrio, their attorney, took six months to order the examination. There was no proper control exercised and I constantly asked when this examination would be scheduled. I finally informed Mr. Carrio that if the examination was not scheduled before the end of the year, I would contact the court. The examination was then scheduled and completed.

In 1990, I visited Doctor Boray, a physician retained and paid for by Mr. Judas' insurance carrier, hired to attack, bring one down with dishonor, undermine and degrade the individual in any mode his devious, darkened mind could conjure. His medical report contained the following statement: "Memory was intact for recent and remote past events. She was oriented to time, place and person." I had informed him that I had toxins in my body, which were being excreted intermittently in the form of pus through the mouth and stool. His report continued: "Miss Sansiviero presents for examination with a fixed belief that she is suffering from a vague disease involving poisons, toxins and infections." Doctor Boray's report continues with the following crowning insult: "These symptoms have intensified and broadened over the past ten years to the point that they have taken on delusional proportions that are not open to reasonable doubt." Everything that I had previously stated and documented fell to the wayside.

In May 1995, a *sophisticated test* was ordered by a Doctor Brown. This test called *Clinical Analysis of Dark Field Scan of Peripheral Blood*, revealed "Clumping of Blood Indicative of Chronic Pain Syndrome. This test definitely indicated the existence of toxins in my system. Low-grade fevers. The stool test definitely indicates that pus exists. Symptoms consistent with blood picture."

Doctors, you must listen to your patients! Speaking to Doctor Boray was the equivalent of speaking to a "brick wall." His medical report was a completely erroneous attack on my belief system, my integrity and my judgment. Why are physicians viewed with distrust by the public? Is it due to the rigidity of their medical minds and their inability to truly listen to their patients? Doctor Boray "thought" he knew what he was doing and that is what made him so dangerous. In his typical approach to my condition, he failed to recognize the totality of the condition of the patient before him. When I asked Doctor Brown what physicians do when they do not have this sophisticated test, he answered, *"They guess."*

THE MYSTIC MASTERS SPEAK (Boulder City, NV: New Life Foundation, 1974, page 252, by Vernon Howard) quotes Leo Tolstoy: *"The worst of human errors spring in most cases from the fact that men who stand on a low intellectual level, when they encounter events of a higher order, instead of trying to rise to the higher level from which these events can be rightly viewed, and making an effort to understand them, judge them by their own low standards, and the less they know of what they speak, the more arrogant and fixed are their judgments."*

Doctors, you must be willing to admit that you might not have all the answers. Otherwise, it retards medical progress and, who knows, you and your family may be that next victim of your own unwillingness to admit to your own weighty mistakes.

Doctor Boray's medical report continues: "Her mother died a slow death at age 79, which Miss Sansiviero found very traumatic. Following the loss, she was unable to work full-time -- " There is a statement dated 1982 in my legal files from my place of employment that I worked full-time following the death of my mother; in fact, I returned to work the day after the funeral. Dr Boray's medical report continues: "She reports an uncomplicated pregnancy and delivery." I was never at any time pregnant. Dr. Boray reluctantly corrected his error, *"She was the product of an uncomplicated pregnancy and delivery."* My mother's pregnancy was never the subject of any discussion.

These are some of the challenges that you will encounter when you come face-to-face with incompetence. Coincidentally, Dr. Boray is still a practicing neurologist. These great difficulties were created by physicians who neglected to communicate with their colleagues and research the problem.

As a result of the *sophisticated test,* Doctor Brown prescribed a substance called *"Scan,"* a combination of organic acids involved in the body's citric acid cycle, which process produced energy from food substances at the mitochondrial level of the cells. I was notified by my treating physician that my insurance company would not cover this experimental treatment. Within a short time after ingesting the "Scan," it caused the severe pains throughout my body to become more acute with a diarrhea-type of action several times a day. By 1995, the distention of my upper and lower stomach had reached enormous proportions but by the end of 1998, following the "Scan" treatment, the distention had completely subsided as a result of an extraordinary amount of secretion of large lumps of pus via stool, coupled with hair-like structure and hardened mucoid material of oval jelly-bean shape covered with pus. Dr. Brown indicated it would take time; it would be slow.

Policy makers we, the public, respectfully but forcefully demand it be mandatory that two witnesses, court stenographer and/or tape recorder be present at *any* meeting of *any* physicians, paid for and retained by *any* insurance company, in order that we, the *unsuspecting public,* will be protected from the following:

    1-   Incompetence.

    2-   Misunderstandings.

    3-   Misquotes.

    4-   Distortion of the facts to serve their own purposes.

    5-   Obvious blundering errors by these

physicians who are reluctant to correct their errors, who abuse and insult the disabled and those reduced to invalid status in any way they deem necessary or the more insidious by nuance and innuendo.

6- Our legitimate complaints being ignored.

7- Dishonor.

8- Their corrupting influence.

Surely this is a viable alternative to protect the *unsuspecting public*. We strongly demand reform; that you not allow the incalculable damages and consequences to remain when you, our policy makers, have an effective means of avoiding such gross errors.

We respect and fully demand this reform be enforced in the very near future.

In 1995, I contacted an attorney in New Jersey in an attempt to retain an expert witness for ethics. He recommended a College Professor who suggested Mr. Raymond, an attorney at the university, who taught legal ethics. Mr. Raymond visited my home and assured me he would listen to the facts, fully aware of my dilemma with Mr. Judas discouraging other attorneys from handling my legal matters. He stated: *"what has happened to you is a tragedy."* He assisted me in retaining counsel. Two attorneys visited my home and agreed to accept <u>ten percent</u> of recovery for trial.

The following are remarks made by Mr. Raymond in his legal statement after Mr. Judas' attempt to discourage him from being an expert witness on my behalf, continuing to state that I was receiving psychiatric treatments and that my case had no merit: "Mr. Judas failed to make an appropriate inquiry into the best forum for vindicating his client's rights. When Mr. Judas appeared before the H.S.A. Panel, he misrepresented his client's condition and treatment in a damaging manner. Specifically, he informed the panel that his client was currently being treated for psychiatric disorders, *an untrue fact.* He thus breached his fiduciary duty of diligence by not depicting his client's condition and treatment; he breached his fiduciary duty of zeal by unnecessarily harming his client; and he breached his fiduciary duty of diligence by failing to recognize false statements by the opposing party."

"Mr. Judas violated his fiduciary duties of confidentiality and loyalty by making negative remarks about his client to other attorneys who contacted him to inquire about her case when she was searching for a lawyer to replace him."

Returning to my treatment and diagnosis,a short time after beginning the "Scan" treatment, the "pulling, drawing and wind" sensation in my head (suggesting a neurological problem) completely subsided. This was followed with the drawing from the front of my head starting at the hairline and continuing over my whole head, with drippings coming down the back of my neck and a *"sensation"* of the drippings dispersing into my back. As this was occurring, the agonizing pains in my head increased in intensity to the point where my entire body shook; this continued for approximately six months and thereafter my imbalance and shaking completely subsided.

Since prior to the time of trial in 1996, after an in-depth examination of my daily log, my physician informed me that the medical problem was caused by the encasement of my brain from the infection of my upper left tooth, and subsequently after taking the Antivert (antihistamine), that caused the "pulling, drawing and the wind" sensation. Diagnosis: *Idiosyncratic responses to medications.* At this point, I recall initially complaining that I felt *"something"* encase my brain and I *"strongly felt"* it was from my left upper tooth. He stated, "You were misdiagnosed because no one bothered to investigate your daily log."

At this point, I was in a most precarious situation. I had experienced indescribable torturous pains in my head and severe pains throughout my entire body, reduced to invalid status for many years, and I now received the confirmation that my medical problem was not conversion hysteria, but the idiosyncratic responses to medications. Two highly regarded medical expert witnesses were willing to testify on my behalf that I was experiencing conversion hysteria whereby I probably would receive a large sum of money. In order to accomplish this,

I would have had to lie under oath regarding my medical problem. This was a challenge to my sense of honor, everything I ever believed in and a compromise against my conscience.

My trial attorneys had informed me when I testified I could not be aggressive in bringing forth Mr. Judas' incompetence, deceptions or professional misconduct inasmuch as he had admitted to liability. I was also advised not to break my silence regarding Mr. Judas who had violated the law and aggressively harassed me for years while I was reduced to invalid status. I believe this illustrates how easy it is to suppress the incompetence and deceptions of attorneys.

A respected attorney strongly advised me to settle the case due to the all-male judiciary. I was not aware that an all-male judiciary was an obstacle to justice for a woman, especially since *"Christ"* treated woman as his equal.

We, the public, are not suggesting the dismantling of our all-male judicial system; we want the dismantling of prejudiced minds in our judicial system, recognizing that unprejudiced minds are a prerequisite to justice. We want unprejudiced minds that will tirelessly pursue authentic justice and with public exposure, we will accomplish the inevitable goal of an unquestionable and genuine justice.

Having been confronted with the inaction of our judicial system on so many levels over so many years, my confidence in the system was thoroughly destroyed. I became aware that simply because the truth was submitted, there was no guarantee that justice would be served.

The attorney of record thereafter submitted a demand for $90,000.00 and I was shocked. A back-and-forth situation continued to exist regarding the settlement. In October of 1995, a demand of $100,000.00 was submitted, and "after" the demand was submitted I inquired if I should request Doctor Gram's widow in Tennessee to forward my "complete" full office medical records to the attorney of record, and he responded "Yes." The records were sent to him in December of 1995 and thereafter he remarked: "I'm glad we didn't settle." Although he did not have his client's full and complete medical records, he simply proceeded without hesitation and made a demand. My cousin, "Monte," later informed me that "the die has already been cast."

In March of 1996, just immediately prior to the time of trial, one of the trial attorneys demanded $100,000; the insurance company offered $90,000 and I settled, because I now had confirmation of my exact medical condition and I did not want to violate the gift of truth for financial gain.

My attorneys of record now aggressively demanded one-third of recovery rather than the agreed upon ten percent. Due to the volume of legal files, I consented to their demand. After all my outstanding bills were paid, there was absolutely no money left. I was later advised by an attorney that I was "lucky" to get anything because it's very hard to sue a lawyer.

I think we must ask ourselves: "If there is anything called justice, why should it be so difficult to sue an attorney if a member of the public has been damaged by his incompetent action or inaction?" This unjust active force must be challenged now; otherwise, there is no justice for any of us.

After thirty-one years and five months following my accident, I no longer suffer from torturous head pains and severe pains throughout my body. I no longer experience "low-grade fevers" and following very sharp pains and pulling in my eyes, I am no longer in need of a magnifying glass when reading. I currently experience no sleeping difficulty because of the absence of pain, which I can only describe as truly an indescribable state of bliss. Although the agonizing, torturous pains have subsided, I still experience the lack of bodily strength and vigor.

So much for the "*absurdity*" of American-Style Justice and the sad illusion of protection by our judicial system from attorney's professional disreputable acts in the absence of prejudicial publicity.

Why am I grateful now? Because I have been given this opportunity to make you all aware how easy it is for us to be wronged by the inaction of our judicial system regarding professional misconduct, and share how you can protect yourself from being victimized.

I view my crisis as an opportunity to assist you! I experienced tremendous deceptions and incompetence during my invalid status and because of my experience I hope to awaken you from your complacency. You must remember, your complacency and apathy towards your legal plight will fly in the face of your claim. If your attitude does not change, you could be placed in a similar situation; you would then be susceptible to tremendous manipulation. Needless to say, there is no equation that ensures justice and, while solutions have yet to be discovered that would ensure justice, you must nevertheless make every effort to protect yourself and your family and thereby diminish your chances of becoming a victim.

For you personally, are there any remedies at your disposal to this underlying problem of our current dysfunctional judicial system? Are there ways you can "attempt" to promote a favorable outcome if you are involved in an accident? Yes, there are remedies -- you must make use of the resources at your disposal. I am making an impassioned plea for you to utilize all means to protect yourself from being abused by those in power within the judicial system. I trust these guidelines will burn in your conscience. The following illustrates some practical and uncomplicated suggestions in the attempt to accomplish a positive outcome. However, if you wish to co-exist with fraud and deception in the legal profession, do not take these suggestions seriously:

   1) If you are involved in an accident
      or any other type of legal situation,
      make sure that you or a member of your
      family has a voice recorder on your
      telephone inasmuch as all conversations
      with your attorney, the legal secretary,
      or anyone involved with your lawsuit

should be recorded. Bear in mind, they indulge in deliberate falsification, so you must therefore utilize all positive assertive energy and positive constructive action.

2) You must always assume your own attorney is the lethal weapon in your legal matter inasmuch as he will inevitably refuse to accept responsibility for his own ineptitude and, believe it or not, use pit-bull tactics.

3) If and when your attorney informs you that the attorney for the opposing party has requested an adjournment, do not assume that is the truth -- they are members of the country club known as the Bar Association. They enjoy lunch and drinks together!

4) If and when you attend a deposition or Examination Before Trial, "demand" that the examination be held at your attorney's office and, again, insist on a tape recorder. You will not be able to bring a tape recorder to court because in 1994, I was advised that a tape recorder was not permitted in the courthouse.

This provokes another question: Why would Our judicial system, supposedly dedicated to the genuine, constant search for truth, object to modern technology in the form of a tape recorder? Having such technology in the courtroom would eliminate an enormous number of errors and would thereby facilitate justice. On the other hand, such technology would force the legal community to be very cautious as to

what they say or do -- this is exactly
what we require in our tainted, biased
judicial system!

5) Utmost in your mind should be the sad
fact that your attorney is for "himself;"
he just doesn't care what your problems
are. If you do not keep abreast of the
entire situation, he will just allow your
case to "slide."

6) Accurate journals are a necessity; as
a matter of fact, you must maintain two
daily logs. If you are not capable of
writing a daily log, dictate what you can
to anyone who will take simple notes for
you. Keep a daily log for all telephone
calls (date, time and to whom you spoke),
what they said, plus your telephone
recordings of all conversations will
confirm everything. Keep another daily
log of everything you are experiencing

(date, time and duration of pain and suffering).

7) Any and all requests must be made to your attorney in writing, "Return Registered Receipt Requested," with a copy for your file. If you do not have such documentation, they will certainly testify under oath with a straight face, without blinking an eye, that they never received your correspondence or telephone request. It is also important that you request, in writing, any documents or copies that your attorney has in his possession.

8) When you have appointments with any physicians, paid for and retained by any insurance company, you must be accompanied by two witnesses with a tape recorder, and/or court stenographer (Demand it! At least until our policy

makers make up their brilliant minds to protect the unsuspecting public.) The basic reason for this security stems from the shocked reaction you will undergo by their medical report with its errors, and ultimately question the reality of the physician's credentials, especially when your complaints are ignored. You must be prepared to be hurled by insurance company physicians into a situation similar to a firing-squad, because their physicians are paid to attack, discredit and undermine you in any way they possibly can and, trust me, they can and will. If they do not perform their task of attack, they will not have a job! They will attack you in every possible way that your "innocent mind" would never even think of. Of course, you may be lucky and come into the presence of an intelligent, sensitive and caring physician but, keep in mind, that also in this rare event of professionalism they are human beings and prone to serious mistakes.

9) Prior to your testifying at a deposition or in court, you must visit a Supreme Courthouse, sit in on a case similar to yours and "listen," but more importantly get a taste of what to expect in your action. Contact the clerk's office and advise them as to what type of case you are interested in. The first-hand knowledge is invaluable. It is simplistic to think these suggestions are a panacea, but they will be very helpful guidelines. If you are prudent, you will not end up shaking your head in disbelief that anyone in our day and

age could have been subjected to such inequity and indignities.

10) In the event that your insurance carrier cancels your no-fault benefits, never under any circumstances, allow your attorney to submit your claim to the no-fault forum, Health Services Association, inasmuch as their decision is final with no right to appeal.

11) If you unfortunately suffer defeat in your proceedings and you have any assets, you will be responsible for all court costs and attorney fees.

12) If, at any time during the course of litigation, you become aware of anything that your attorney has done which is less than competent or less than honorable, do not sign what is called the "General Release" because

once you sign that document, you would limit your ability to sue your attorney for malpractice. Be sure to seek the advice of a paralegal relating to the stipulation that must be included in the document. You must realize that your attorney would not advise you regarding that stipulation -- he is out to protect himself, not you!

13) If you are sixty-five or completely disabled with absolutely no income, request in writing, that your attorney submit what is called "Special Preference" for an immediate trial, making sure that the envelope designates "Return Registered Receipt Requested."

An additional note, I have had the pleasure of knowing competent legal secretaries in various law offices, and they have all indicated that attorneys elongate their work to bill the insurance company a larger sum, and we pay the price with our higher premiums. They do this and more with no integrity and pure greed.

14) On numerous occasions, I overheard conversations between attorneys, who should be representing us, and an attorney for the insurance company, e.g., "If you push to settle this case for us, we will give you work out of our office," meaning the insurance company. Your attorney then informs you that you have a very weak case and you should settle. Your attorney then increases his income by working for the insurance company who is supposed to compensate you for your pain and suffering.

Being aware of the aforementioned guidelines you now cannot claim ignorance of the truth. You must remain strong and not despair, *because there are brilliant physicians who do care and will assist you. Just keep going!*

* * *

APPENDIX

This additional information pertains to the policy makers of our nation regarding prayers in our schools.

* * *

Decent citizens of the United States, let us band together, stand up and raise our voices -- blast our policy makers.

For many decades our nation very successfully practiced the separation of "church and state," coupled with prayers in our schools and colleges. We had violence-free schools and never needed bouncers. Policy makers of our country, please consider the following questions carefully:

A. If we bombard our children with violence, shouldn't you be aware that at some point it would affect their behavior?

B. If we expose our children to an atmosphere of correct principles and to "ANY PRAYER" that elevates the consciousness, a large percentage of our children would act accordingly without the millions of dollars spent on the cost and the laughable necessity of security systems, bouncers and/or private police officers in our school systems.

A brilliant mind is not required to realize what has happened to our youth since prayers within our public schools have been eliminated. A consensus of the population has revealed that most Americans want PRAYERS back in our schools and institutions of higher learning. In essence, why should the "loud" minority force the "silent" majority to change their practice because they "might" be offended?

We should not care that their *"small minds"* have been offended, and ask them to just walk alone in some of the neighborhoods during the early evening hours; they will then understand the true meaning of being offended.

Unless this reform is mandated in an effort to guide our youth toward correct principals, our schools and institutions of higher learning will be giving diplomas to skillful barbarians.

We must recognize the diabolical nature of the policy makers within our country who freely acknowledge the devil worship in our jails, bringing forth the unspeakable negative energies upon our beloved country

-- And *"PRAYERS"* are banned from our schools!

We want the jail inmates to have rights, but they definitely should not have the right to bring forth even more negativity upon our nation than they already have by their unlawful behavior.

We must loudly cry out and demand that policy makers bring an end to this *satanic influence* in our prisons, better known as *National Homicide*. Undoubtedly, our brilliant policy makers know their influences and can bring forth negative energies upon you, your family, and our beloved nation.

What else can we, *"the public-majority"* say to our policy makers to let them know we don't like it?

* * *

Due to the inaction of our judicial system regarding professional misconduct, and being aware of the legal time limit, the author of this book was literally forced to *"personally"* initiate litigation against her incompetent attorney. Therefore, the author feels obliged to share the knowledge gained regarding the rules, regulations and suggestions necessary for such litigation.

* * *

HOW TO LITIGATE AGAINST AN INCOMPETENT ATTORNEY

1. Purchase the book titled "Simon's New York Code of Professional Responsibility, Annotated 1995-1996," from Lawyer's Cooperative Publishing, Aqueduct Building, Rochester, New York 14603. Tel no. 1-800-307-8140.

2. Place an ad in your local newspaper for an experienced, knowledgeable and competent legal stenographer to assist you. (If your finances permit, also seek advice from a paralegal, visit a law library and investigate other cases of legal malpractice.)

3. Before you initiate litigation, be sure that you have absolutely no assets (property or monies) because if you do not win the litigation, you will be liable for all the court and attorney's fees for both sides. Check with the Clerk of the Appellate Division in your state regarding the statute of limitations. For example, in New York State, you have three years to institute litigation against your attorney for legal malpractice.

4. Make an original and three copies of every legal form.

5. Purchase the following forms from a stationery store, specializing in legal forms:

   a. Form B-106, Summons with Notice (Refer to Format #1A)

   b. T-442 Demand for Production of Insurance Agreements (Refer to Format #2)

   c. B-438, Notice to Take Deposition Upon Oral Examination (Refer to Format #3)

   d. B-69, Subpoena Duces Tecum, (Refer to Format #4)

   e. Purchase a box of printed Blue-Backs (Refer to Format #5)

   f. Note of Issue (Statement of Readiness) (Refer to Format #6)

g. Change of Venue (Refer to Format #8)

6. Attach the Verified Complaint (Refer to Format #1B) to the back of the Summons with Notice, which is Format #1A. Cover the back of these two legal documents with a Blue-Back filling in the necessary information (Refer to Attached Blue-Back Format #5). Then fold the top of the Blue-Back approximately one inch at the top in order that one inch of the Blue-Back will show on the front of the Summons with Notice.

7. Both forms, the Summons with Notice and the Verified Complaint, require an Index Number, which must be purchased at the County Clerk's Office in the county of trial. At that time, serve the original Summons with Notice and the Verified Complaint with the County Clerk (Submit the original to the County Clerk).

8. Contact a process server in your community (listed in the Yellow Pages or online), and the process server will serve a Summons upon the defendant (the attorney you are suing), together with a Verified Complaint and the obligation of submitting the Proof of Service to the County Clerk. Discuss with the process server as to the requirements regarding the amount of monies necessary, etc.

9. You will receive a Demand for a Verified Bill of Particulars and you will generally have twenty (20) days to comply.

10. Prepare a Verified Bill of Particulars (Refer to Format #7)

11. Forward the original Verified Bill of Particulars to the Clerk of the Court in the county where the trial will be

held. Send one copy to the attorney representing your attorney, providing "Return Registered Receipt Requested" on the envelope. Needless to say, retain a copy.

12. Prepare a Notice of Discovery and Inspection (Refer to Format #9).

13. Prepare a Demand for Production of Insurance Agreements (Refer to Format #2).

14. Send a Written Demand for your complete file, ensuring that your envelope contains the words "Return Registered Receipt Requested."

If the attorney you are suing does not respond within a reasonable time, have the legal secretary type an Order for you (Refer to Format #10).

15. Send out "Notice to Take Examination upon Oral Examination," (Refer to Format #3). Contact the attorney representing the lawyer you are suing for a suitable date for the Examination Before Trial.

16. Basic questions for the Examination Before Trial (Refer to Format #3B). Bring a tape recording device. Demand that Examination Before Trial be held at an attorney's office rather than the court inasmuch as your judicial system does not allow tape recorders. Contact a stenotype school in your area for a soon-to-be court stenographer and a notary public, especially if you are not able to afford an experienced court room stenographer; Ensuring that the tape recorder is used whether or not the court reporter agrees in order to eliminate any and all possible errors;

instruct the court reporter that the transcript must be submitted to you within a month.

17. When the typed transcript of the Examination Before Trial is received, check it very carefully against the tape recording. Send the original of the E.B.T. to the Clerk of the Supreme Court where the trial will be held with a covering letter, e.g., "Enclosed please find Examination Before Trial..." Include the index number and, remember, the envelope must read "Return Registered Receipt Requested." Submit one copy of the E.B.T. to the attorney representing the attorney you are instituting legal proceedings against with a covering letter (Refer to above), remembering the envelope must indicate" Return Registered Receipt Requested".

18. Contact a nearby law university or college requesting the name of an attorney who teaches ethics in an attempt to retain him as an expert witness. In addition, also inquire if he knows any attorneys who could handle a legal malpractice trial against your attorney. Be prepared for that individual to make attempts to protect the attorney you are suing. Better yet, handle it yourself! It doesn't take literary talent to submit the truth.

19. Bear in mind, no one knows the case better than "you," because you have lived it.

20. Type a Certificate of Readiness (Refer to Format #6), and bring this certificate to the Supreme Court Clerk's Office wherein the Clerk will give you a calendar number.

21. Prepare Form B-69, Subpoena Duces Tecum, for every witness you wish to have appear and testify, ensuring that every name and address is correct. Contact the clerk's office in the county where the trial is scheduled to be held and insert the trial date. In the upper right-hand corner of the form, add "We will advise you as to the exact date of this trial."

22. Contact the process server as to the amount of money that must be included for each subpoena - - it will be a nominal fee.

23. In the event that you feel you will not receive a fair trial because your attorney is well-known in your area, you may request a "Change of Venue," meaning a "Change of County." (Refer to Format #8).

24. Contact the media, if you wish, since by doing so you will be giving awareness to your fellow man.

25. Bear in mind that few attorneys possess the perfection of an expert so you, yourself, will not be doing any worse than most attorneys in the field.

* * *

Notes

<u>Notes</u>

Printed in the United States
By Bookmasters